The Br
in The
Vis
D0997902

How to survive and succeed with

an interactive whiteboard

Greg Braham

Acknowledgements

I should like to thank Karen for recognising the value of allowing me to 'play' and for her patience and support throughout this time.

I should also like to thank Erin and Sam for keeping me company during the long hours of research and for introducing me to the joys of the Ballamory and Postman Pat websites.

Finally, I should like to thank the children I have taught, whose curiosity and imagination have inspired me to prepare creative lessons.

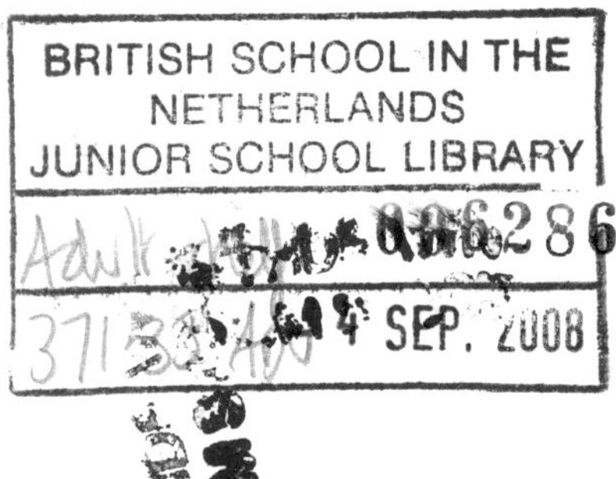
BRITISH SCHOOL IN THE NETHERLANDS JUNIOR SCHOOL LIBRARY
SEP. 2008

Permission to Photocopy
This book contains materials which may be reproduced by photocopier or other means for use by the purchaser. The permission is granted on the understanding that these copies will be used within the educational establishment of the purchaser. The book and all its contents remain copyright. Copies may be made without reference to the publisher or the licensing scheme for the making of photocopies operated by the Publishers' Licensing Agency.

The right of Greg Braham to be identified as the author of this work has been asserted by him in accordance with sections 77 and 78 of the Copyright, Designs and Patents Act 1988.

How to survive and succeed with an interactive whiteboard
MT10002
ISBN-13: 978 1 85503 403 7
© Greg Braham
Illustrations © Rebecca Barnes
All rights reserved
First published 2006
Reprinted 2007

Printed in the UK for LDA
Abbeygate House, East Road, Cambridge, CB1 1DB, UK

Contents

Contents

Introduction

As I sit here preparing to write this introduction, I feel as I did when I was first confronted with an interactive whiteboard (IWB). I know that there is a wealth of opportunities open to me from this point onwards, but I feel a bit daunted. Perhaps this is how you feel with your IWB too. I suppose the best place to start for each of us is at the beginning. Then it's up to me to help you to take some small steps and to help those steps become confident strides.

Looking back, that is pretty much what I have done since entering teaching. Initially very negative about my own teaching abilities, after completing my NQT year I gained in confidence and have now taught in a wide range of year groups. I have always enjoyed using computers and have brought my expertise to the schools I have worked in. Over that time, there has been a huge development, in both the presence of ICT in schools and its use in teachers' lessons. There have been a range of developments in the past few years: from a small number of computers in schools, to the installation of ICT suites, to banks of laptops and palm pads purchased for children's use, to wireless networking to give more flexible use of ICT and, most recently, the introduction of IWBs.

"I recommend a range of interactive whiteboard activities."

For me, the IWB is one of the most exciting developments in ICT in schools, and it has had a significant impact on my teaching. Some argue that it is an expensive overhead projector (OHP). I disagree completely, and say that the only reason they are seen in this way is a lack of appropriate training and support. You'll find the forthcoming chapters full of ideas, tips, hints and, most importantly, support and advice, so that by the end of the book you'll feel as passionate about the potential of IWBs as I do.

If you are considering getting IWBs in your school, I suggest you read this book from the beginning. You will find all the advice you need. If you are further on in the process and have an IWB already, I still suggest that you start at the beginning to iron out any areas of confusion or misunderstanding.

The IWB is a superb resource in skilled hands. As a qualified teacher, you already have the skills to develop, motivate and educate the children in your class. The IWB offers you a very powerful set of creative tools to work with which can help you to support all children in your care.

My hope is that this book will be a well-thumbed practical resource that will inspire you, offer you food for thought, and help you to develop the way you teach.

We offer a list of websites on pages 54–64 that are intended to be used as you develop your skills with your IWB. The websites included provide a wealth of activities, downloadable resources and guidance. All were available at the time of going to press. The publisher is not responsible for the content of any of these websites.

Chapter 1 Deciding on an interactive whiteboard

Why use an interactive whiteboard?

Research & Evaluation of Interactive, Electronic Whiteboards, based at Cascade, The University of Hull, 2002

The REVIEW Project has found that teachers and pupils identify the following benefits in having an IWB in their classroom.

- *Motivation.* A greater sense of motivation was noted. Teachers' motivation stemmed from the huge amount of teaching materials made available to them. Pupil motivation was linked to the visual appeal of the board and the increased sense of involvement that they felt they had.
- *Use of colour.* Many pupils commented that greater use of colour helped them to master concepts and link ideas.
- *Use of multimedia.* Both pupils and teachers commented favourably upon the use of video, sound and images.
- *Screen interactivity.* Both teachers and pupils enjoyed the system's interactive nature. This increased the child's involvement and made it quick and easy for teachers to prepare activities.
- *Saving and retrieving resources.* Teachers were able to develop a bank of resources that was easily accessible and could be shared with colleagues.

With such benefits apparent, we begin this chapter by looking at how to bring the IWB into your classroom and school.

Developing a plan

If you are in the fortunate position of being involved in the acquisition of IWBs for your school, you are at an exciting moment. You are about to embark on something engaging and possibly even life changing for the staff, the children, and the teaching and learning in your school.

Choosing the right type of IWB is a frightening proposition – it involves spending a lot of money, and there are many decisions to be made. Start by thinking about your staff and how confident you think they will be about working with this new technology. This, along with the cost implications and any possibility of external funding or support, will influence how you organise your purchasing plan. Here are a few questions to consider to start the process:

- Can you afford to install an IWB in every classroom?
- If not, can you afford a data projector to project images from a computer onto a standard whiteboard for each class, or will there be only one in each year group to start with?
- If you can afford a data projector for each class, can you afford to phase IWBs into year groups?
- If you are phasing in the IWBs, how will this be best managed?

If you choose to phase in boards, your approach will depend on your circumstances. You could start at the younger end of the school and introduce IWBs into successive year groups so that the children go through the school with them. If a key factor is staff confidence and motivation, you may start with the most ICT-literate members of staff.

The following sections will give you more to think about. The REVIEW Project has conducted a large amount of research on IWBs. Their website has some sound advice for schools considering purchasing IWBs.

www.thereviewproject.org

Choosing the best interactive whiteboard for you

IWBs come in a wide range of sizes and types from a large number of manufacturers. Below are basic outlines of the different IWBs available.

Infrared/ultrasound solutions

These tend to be the most portable systems, and consist of a receiver that attaches to any flat surface or existing dry-wipe board. This receives information from a computer, which it projects onto your chosen surface. You can interact with the board using pens that communicate with the receiver. This system can be set up and taken down quite quickly.

- *Advantages*. This option is less expensive than other solutions. The receiver is portable and very easy to set up.
- *Disadvantages*. The receiver can fall off the board/wall. It is a less robust option than the other solutions. The pens can be large and may be hard for younger children or those with special needs to hold.

Mimio:
www.mimio.com
E-Beam:
www.luidiauk.com
www.e-beam.com

Touch-sensitive boards

These boards are made of two soft sheets of material with a narrow gap between them. When touched by an IWB pen or a fingertip, the sheets make contact with each other. This contact is registered by the board's software, and the computer that is linked to the board carries out appropriate actions.

- *Advantages*. Easy to use – young children and those with special needs are able to use the board as various things can be used to control it: a fingertip, a pointer, the board's pens and so on. They are more robust than infrared/ultrasound.
- *Disadvantage*. More expensive than infrared/ultrasound.

SMART Board:
www.smarttech.com or
www.smart-uk.co.uk

Magnetic-resistance boards

These boards have a hard surface that covers a grid of copper wire. When an IWB pen or stylus is used, the board's software registers where magnetic connections are made on the surface and reacts appropriately.

- *Advantages*. A very robust option. Young children can use the pen or stylus, as it is a good size.
- *Disadvantage*. More expensive than infrared/ultrasound.

Activboard:
www.prometheanworld.com

RMClassboard:
www.rm.com

Once you have decided on the most appropriate type of IWB, you will need to choose the size you want. The size is the diagonal measurement from corner to corner and is generally given in inches. On the whole, the larger the board, the larger you can display the laptop or PC screen that the board is linked to. Obviously, it is vital that children can clearly see the text or images.

Installation options

Having decided on the number, type and size of IWB, you are faced with further options, the next being to do with installation.

Free-standing boards

These tend to be smaller, and have two supports that slot into brackets on the back of the board and enable it to stand on a flat surface. They can be carried in and out of classrooms and set up and linked to a computer relatively quickly and easily, on a tabletop or other suitable flat surface.

These types of board tend to be too small for whole-class use, and are more useful for presentations, meetings or work in small groups.

"You have ten minutes to assemble this interactive whiteboard, starting from now."

Boards on mobile stands

These boards are larger and are permanently set up on a stand with casters. The board can be moved from one location to another with relative ease. If you have more than one floor or narrow corridors, moving it will be an issue.

This type of solution is good in principle if you don't have the budget to buy a large number of IWBs. In practice, you will often find that only the confident staff end up using it. It takes time to move and set everything up. The projector and IWB need to be aligned correctly for the projected image to be seen clearly. If the projector is knocked, this alignment can be lost, resulting in time being needed to realign the board. Lastly, you are likely to have trailing leads on the floor with this system, raising health and safety issues.

Fixed-position boards

This solution has the IWB, and ideally the projector, permanently mounted in the classroom, enabling staff to use the board on a daily basis. This is dependent on a larger amount of funding being available, but is the most effective way of making staff comfortable with the technology in the shortest possible time.

The fixed position option also saves time. If you have a mobile board of some form, setting up may take around ten minutes. Most importantly, having an IWB set up permanently in each classroom means that staff are able to use the board spontaneously.

This will be the approach that I address in this book, although much of what I say will relate to the other options mentioned.

Positioning your interactive whiteboard

It is vital that sufficient thought is given to the placement of the IWB in order to maximise its accessibility. This is likely to be in a central position so that it is visible from all parts of the room. IWBs increase the amount of discussion, so try to ensure that the children can see each other. The IWB should be at a height that enables the teacher to access all areas of it. It will need to be high enough to be visible to all, yet low enough to allow children to reach most of the board. For health and safety reasons, you should not allow children to use platforms to access higher areas, so it is important to position it correctly from the start. Fixing a board about 80 cm from the floor in Key Stage 1 and 80–90 cm from the floor in Key Stage 2 seems to work well. You may find that your boards need to be lower than this, especially if some children have problems with mobility and reach. Boards can be set up with the teacher's options at the top of the board and the pupil options at the bottom.

Whichever projector(s) you buy, try to clean the filters every few weeks to increase the lifespan of the bulbs.

Make sure that there is room to stand on either side of the IWB to accommodate right- and left-handed writers. This also enables users to stand clear of the glare from the projector. A clear route to the IWB for users is important.

Keep a space in front of the IWB free for a few chairs for small-group work. A carpeted area is good for younger children.

A computer needs to be linked to the IWB. While needing to be close enough to the IWB to connect to it via the supplied cables, it does not need to be right next to it. You can use a remote keyboard, which the children can also operate. A laptop will enable you to prepare resources away from the classroom and link up with your whiteboard afterwards.

You need to consider the lighting in the room too, as this affects how clearly the images on the board can be seen. Will the board have the sun shining on it at any point in the day? If so, blinds or curtains will be needed. The darker the blinds, the better.

While considering light sources, think about the projector. There are hundreds of projectors on the market and your choice will depend on your circumstances. Consider the following:

- The size of the room.
- The required image size – this will affect the distance from the board that the projector will need to be fixed, which in turn influences the choice of projector because of its maximum and minimum *image-throw distance*.
- The brightness of the bulb (measured in ANSI lumens – somewhere between 1,000 and 1,500 lumens should be sufficient for most classrooms).

Image-throw distance. The maximum and minimum distance a projector can be fixed from the screen. Too close and the image may be out of focus or not fill the screen; too far away and the image may be too large for the screen.

Whichever projector(s) you buy, try to clean the filters every few weeks to increase the lifespan of the bulbs; they are expensive to replace.

There are possible health and safety issues associated with IWBs:

> Tests carried out by the National Radiological Protection Board have shown that the peripheral vision of IWB users may be harmed even when they are not looking directly into the beam of the projector.
>
> *Child Education* (March 2005)

Owing to the short time they have been in use, no conclusive evidence has been found. However, it must be made clear that users should not stare directly into the beam of the projector. When facing the class, users should stand to one side of the board, ensuring that they are out of the glare of the beam.

When installing your IWB, try to make sure that the computer controlling it is linked to the Internet and to your school's network system.

Becta (British Educational Communications and Technology Agency) have issued a statement on their website:

> It is recommended that health and safety notices are posted adjacent to interactive whiteboards; although the content or posting of such notices is not a requirement under law, it should be considered as best practice.

With regard to health and safety, there is a photocopiable poster on page 53.

National Whiteboard Network: www.nwnet.org.uk

Becta: www.becta.org.uk

Additional advice can be found on the websites of the National Whiteboard Network and Becta.

Internet and network access

When installing your IWB, try to make sure that the computer controlling it is linked to the Internet and to your school's network system. Being linked to the school's network means that all staff have access and can share resources they have developed. This cuts down on workload and is an excellent way to build confidence. Having Internet access opens up the classroom to a wealth of possibilities, including on-the-spot research by children, access to websites to support teaching points and the use of resources such as film clips and sound files. This will be covered in later chapters. If you don't have this facility at the moment, extending network access will add to the cost of installation. However, it will provide dividends later.

Peripherals to enhance your interactive whiteboard

You are now, hopefully, on the way to having an IWB in each classroom. You can make use of a computer's ability to play music, videos, animations and so on. A list of other pieces of hardware that will enhance your IWB follows. The first four items should be given priority.

Speakers

If sound and film clips are going to be used, speakers are essential. Using the projector's in-built speaker tends to be ineffectual. I recommend a pair of speakers mounted above the board, angled down slightly to ensure they carry across the room.

Scanner

A scanner connected to the computer or laptop enables children's work to be scanned in a lesson and displayed instantly on the IWB. It can then be annotated using the IWB's notebook software. This is a strongly motivating factor for children and a great way to bring assessment-for-learning strategies into your plenaries. Appropriate quality scanners are cheap and buying in bulk often earns you a discount.

Video and/or DVD player

The data projector can be switched to project from a video and/or DVD player as well as from the computer. Make sure you know beforehand how to switch between the two channels on your projector.

It is possible to convert video clips into *mpeg* or *avi* files which can be stored digitally on the school's network, meaning that staff would not need to switch the projector image between computer and video when wanting to show something. These files can be easily loaded and played through the PC or laptop using the free Media Player that comes with Windows.

> ***mpeg.*** Moving Pictures Expert Group: a working group that sets international standards for digital video and audio files.
>
> ***avi.*** Audio Video Interleave: a format used to save video and audio digitally.
>
> Simply put, these are two file extensions that show that the file has digital audio or video content.

Remember that the original producer of the video has copyright over the material on the video cassette. There would be definite implications if you were to transfer a television programme, film or other professionally produced material into mpeg or avi format. This method is however ideal to transfer previously recorded VHS or Hi8 video footage shot on older video cameras in order to maintain quality and to aid use within the classroom.

Most laptops can now play DVDs as a standard feature.

Remote-control devices

You can purchase a range of devices that will enable you to control your IWB from anywhere in the room. This means you are not tied to the computer or IWB. The main types are listed below:

- *Wireless keyboards*. These enable alphanumeric text to be entered when not at the computer.
- *Gyromouse*. A wireless mouse that can be used to control the on-screen cursor when not at the board.
- *Interactive pads or tablets*. For example, RM's ClassPad or Promethean's ACTIVslate; roughly A4 in size, these screens come with a stylus that is used to control the on-screen cursor by touching the pad's surface in the corresponding position. These take some getting used to, and can be difficult for younger children to manage effectively. Remember that interactivity should not detract from the pace of a lesson.
- *Voting devices*. These wireless devices are voting pads that allow children to answer questions by choosing from a range of answers. The associated

"I think you might find this helpful."

software can produce graphs and tables to show responses and also track the responses from each device so that teachers can assess each child's understanding. If they are outside your price range, the tried-and-tested mini dry-wipe board and marker pen works nearly as well.

Additional resources

Digital stills cameras

As the cost of digital stills cameras comes down, their accessibility to schools has risen. I recommend investing in a number of child-friendly digital stills cameras so that children can use them in groups. Most cameras of this type connect to a computer via a *USB* cable whereby stored pictures can be *downloaded* quickly and easily. Other such cameras allow children to take pictures directly onto a floppy disk or CD-ROM, so the images can be accessed immediately from one of the computer's disk drives with no need to download them first.

USB. Universal Serial Bus: a way of connecting devices such as cameras, microscopes and storage disks to a computer quickly and sending information to and from that device at speed.

Downloading. Transferring (data or programs) from a server or host computer to your own computer or device. Simply put, the act of getting something onto your computer from somewhere else.

Digital video cameras

The cost of digital video cameras is dropping all the time, and they are becoming more widespread in schools. A cheap option is Intel's Digital Blue Camera, which takes low-resolution video footage and can be used very easily by children. The camera can be used while attached to a computer; or used separately and then reconnected later, using the camera's docking base – enabling the video to be quickly and easily downloaded and projected on the IWB. This camera's software enables you to take photographs and create stop-animation videos. Perfect for Wallace and Gromit fans!

Other, higher-quality video cameras are available. They often come with tripods, microphones and other useful accessories. These cameras need to transfer a lot of information to the PC when downloading the video footage, so it is useful to have on your PC another type of connection called *Firewire* or *IEEE 1394*. If you don't have a Firewire card already installed, they can be purchased and easily fitted on most machines. Newer machines often come with a Firewire port as standard.

Firewire / IEEE 1394. A standard developed by Apple to transfer large amounts of information quickly. This requires a special cable and port or socket on your computer.

As well as special ports, some form of video-editing software helps to cut out any footage that isn't needed and to create a finished product. Windows XP comes with a free piece of software called Windows Movie Maker, which is ideal for this. You can buy products that do the same thing but are more powerful. If you are using Movie Maker, I recommend downloading the latest upgrade from Microsoft's website. Digital video cameras are being used more as schools consider ways in which pupils may record their work; a digital video camera is excellent in PE, for example.

Microsoft: www.microsoft.com

Digital microscopes

All schools in the UK received an Intel digital microscope free a few years ago. Many of them haven't seen the outside of a resource cupboard since. They are good for use in whole-class situations as the IWB allows all the children to see what is happening. You can take photos and video with it, as well as leaving it running and setting it up to take time-lapse photographs when you are away from it. I've used a digital microscope to examine and photograph mould we had grown on bread, and also to make a video of *Daphnia* collected from the school pond.

Visualisers

Visualisers are digital cameras on flexible necks that can be used to display images of 3-D objects, documents and even microscopic images on the IWB. Use them to take an image of a child's work quickly, which can then be shown on the IWB. The work can be annotated on the board, and a picture of this can be taken with the board's software as a record. Visualisers are quicker than scanners, but the cost of supplying every class with one will be high.

Web cams

As broadband becomes more common in schools, web cams become a more viable tool in the classroom.

A web cam is a camera that connects to the laptop or computer and can be used to transfer sound and images from the user to a viewer in a different location. As well as a web cam, you need a computer (three to four years old at most for best results), appropriate software which can often be downloaded for free from the Internet, and a fast connection to the Internet.

Web cams can be purchased very cheaply. The cheaper ones tend not to capture sound and images as well as the slightly more expensive ones. Ideally, the web cam should have a tripod or some other way of stabilising it. Thought should be given to whether the camera's microphone (if it has one) is good enough to record the person speaking or if additional microphones need to be purchased. Once connected, a web cam can open up the classroom to the outside world. It enables children with special needs to communicate more easily with others as there is no need for typed or written communication, as in e-mails and letters.

As broadband becomes more common in schools, web cams become a more viable tool in the classroom. I have included more thoughts on using them in Chapter 6.

Web cams are not as difficult to work as you may think. They offer children a way to share their learning with peers and others from around the world. They enable your children to discuss their experiences of home and school life with other children in a completely different village, town or country.

Geography, science, art and literacy spring to mind when thinking about using a web cam. You will have many ideas in relation to your own topics. You may be able to find a scientist who would be willing to talk to the children via a web-chat, sharing their experiences and knowledge. An author or artist may be willing to show the children how they work in their study or studio and answer their questions.

The speaking and listening requirements for using this resource are clear, and children can use it to share their thoughts, experiences and lives in general. They can learn a great deal visually and aurally without the necessity of visiting a specific location, which may be impractical or even impossible.

Remember that any work using web cams should be well planned. The technology must fade into the background and not hinder the children's abilities to learn from the lessons. The Internet connection at both ends needs to be as fast as possible; having broadband is a real blessing for this type of work. It is important to consider how you are going to organise the children as with web cams only one or two children will be able to fit into the frame at a time. If you wish to use them with large groups or even the whole class, a more professional, and therefore more expensive, solution is needed.

With a solid foundation of understanding and planning in place, we shall move on to more specific classroom concerns. Before that, here are some thoughts from someone who has gone through the choices discussed so far.

Diary

Notes from the front line – the ICT manager

24 November

Fantastic news, the LEA are funding interactive whiteboards in schools and it sounds like we might be getting at least one! Even more fantastic news, after much badgering, persuading and cajoling by myself and the ICT technician, the head teacher has possibly managed to find enough money to fund installation of boards in the remaining classrooms.

27 November

Finally found the painkillers and my headache appears to be subsiding slightly after the meeting I've just had. Who'd have thought there were so many things to consider about getting an IWB? What type of board do we want? What are the benefits of each? What projector do we want? How bright are they? What sort of scanner do we want? Do we really need them? Do we want speakers? Who's going to install the kit? When can they do it? How much will it all cost?

Cost, cost, cost, cost, cost! And doesn't it just!

Still, we are definitely among the lucky ones – eight IWBs will be coming our way next term, all classes installed and able to access the Internet and network – excellent!

Now, how am I going to break it to the staff that they are going to lose their dry-wipe boards?

Chapter 2
Interactive whiteboard basics

The interactive whiteboard as the primary teaching tool

The day you first turn on your IWB is similar to the one when you bring a baby home for the first time. What do you do with it? How do you look after it properly? What if you do something wrong? In this chapter, I hope to assuage some of those fears and help you to develop your confidence.

There is a wide range of issues and considerations to be made when installing an IWB. As we have seen, it should be in as central a location in your classroom as possible. In general, it will be where the dry-wipe board has been, but this may not be practical. For example, one class I visited had the dry-wipe board above a radiator, where the children would have been unable to reach it.

As teachers, we are aware of the issues associated with classroom organisation. Schools are all different and there will be a range of preferences and influences when it comes to classroom layouts. However, if it is to be used to its full potential, the IWB should be considered as the primary tool for supporting your teaching. It needs the primary position in your classroom.

In order to promote the IWB's use, I recommend that the dry-wipe board is removed from the classroom. Keep a standard flipchart for emergencies and in case of technical difficulties with the IWB. If this is not possible or desirable, installing the IWB where the original board was, cutting the dry-wipe board down in size and repositioning it to the side of the IWB should provide reassurance while ensuring that the IWB is the primary board used. When you feel more confident, remove the dry-wipe board and go with the flipchart.

"Don't worry, you'll be fine without it."

It may be a daunting prospect to lose the traditional board. As a compromise, you could keep the dry-wipe boards in storage and promise that any staff who really struggle with the flipchart and the IWB can have the dry-wipe board cut down and returned to their classroom. In my experience, within two weeks all staff will be at ease with their IWB and cease to mention the traditional boards.

Getting to grips with the basic interactive whiteboard functions

Persevere, and within a short time you will start to wonder how you ever managed before. Your IWB, computer and projector combination is everything a traditional board is, and more. It is an OHP, a television screen and even a picture gallery. It is a tool for writing, drawing and typing; and for displaying, presenting and annotating. Knowing the potential of your IWB is the first step towards harnessing it. Next I will explain the four main modes that are commonly associated with it.

.pdf. Portable Document Format: a file format developed by Adobe Systems that allows files created in different applications to be viewed on screen as intended. To read files with a .pdf extension you need Adobe Acrobat Reader – a free piece of software to download from www.adobe.com.

www.cutepdf.com is a piece of software that can be downloaded which will enable you to make your worksheets into .pdf files that will appear exactly as you made them on any computer.

.html. HyperText Markup Language: the language used to create web pages. A .html extension to a file tells you that it has been written in this language.

www.adobe.com
www.cutepdf.com

Pointer mode

In pointer mode, your IWB replaces the mouse and keyboard on your computer or laptop. All actions (clicks, menu selections, writing and drawing, printing, saving and so on) are performed at the board, so you can still face the class. The IWB's virtual keyboard can be used for entering alphanumeric characters – but this can be slow, so is best done in small amounts. Having a wireless keyboard that can be passed around and used by the children overcomes this and also develops interactivity.

An example of using the IWB in this mode is for presentations in programs such as PowerPoint. Advancing the presentation can be done with a touch of the board, and the board's pens can be used to highlight and annotate the information on screen. It is possible to save these annotations and print them, or to save them in a different file format such as *.pdf* or *.html* so they can used in other programs.

A word of warning

It is all too easy to get into the routine of using PowerPoint for everything you do. The animations, sound effects and wow factor help to make it a favourite program with children, but be careful. Too much PowerPoint can make you ill, or at least jaded. I find PowerPoint presentations are generally too linear in their structure. They are great to make one quick point or to focus on one small thing, but if you want to create real interaction between yourself, the class and the board, spend time exploring the board's software. You will find that it gives you the potential to be far more creative in your teaching than PowerPoint can.

Flipchart mode

The most common way to start is to treat the IWB like a traditional board, and use it to scribe on. All boards have some form of flipchart software in which pages can be created. It is possible to move backwards and forwards within this. At the start of the day, the date can be written with an IWB pen or typed using a keyboard on the front page, and any instructions for the class to follow during the registration time can be displayed. The following pages could show the aims and success criteria for the day's lessons, along with resources such as text, pictures and *hyperlinks* to video clips, images or sound clips, other programs such as PowerPoint, or website *URLs* that will support the teaching for the day. For example, a lesson I taught on the water cycle included a link to a lesson task created in Word.

Hyperlinks. Some IWB software allows you to create links between text or images and another file or program on your computer. When the hyperlink icon is selected, the program automatically starts. This is great for reinforcing concepts or teaching points with a PowerPoint presentation or video clip and so on.

URL. Universal Resource Locator: the unique website address that belongs to a site you visit on the Internet.

www.macromedia.com

Before exploring video and animation files from the Internet, download the latest version of Macromedia Flash and Shockwave to enable your computer to play these files.

Leave blank pages in the flipchart to use when you want to gather ideas, make notes or interact in some other way with the class. It is very simple to add further pages at any point if needed.

One of the best things about using the IWB is that whatever you do can be saved on your computer or laptop and opened again later, added to if necessary and then resaved. The work you do today can be used tomorrow, next week, next month and, best of all, next year – saving you work when preparing lessons. Additionally, useful resources can be shared with other staff in your school and reused. That's something you couldn't do with your traditional board.

Have a go!

Try setting up a few pages in a flipchart on your IWB so that you are ready to use the board when next with your class.

On the front page, using the IWB pen, write the date of your next lesson and a message to greet the children. If you are happy with how it looks, then keep it; otherwise use the IWB's board rubber to get rid of it and start again. Once you have set up the front page, add a second. This one could have the aim for the first lesson of the day. Write the aim using the IWB pen, perhaps choosing a different colour. This time, try out your board's handwriting recognition software and change your handwritten aim into a typed one.

This is a good way to encourage clear handwriting and correct letter formation with your children. IWB handwriting recognition software won't always recognise what has been written if the letters are not clearly formed.

Colour. Note that some colours do not work well together – yellow, orange and lime green do not work well on a white background. Remember the possible colour-blind boys. If the children are going to be looking at the board for a long time, consider softening the white background by using a light lilac colour or something similar. Tinted backgrounds are helpful to children with dyslexia.

Finally, use a third page to do some work with the children in the next lesson. You could use it for a mind map or to brainstorm ideas for some shared writing, or simply to jot down discussion notes for later reference.

It is easy to copy and paste images or pictures into your flipchart, so try finding an image to spark off a discussion from the computer's clipart files or perhaps from the Internet.

Tip: copying and pasting images

Working at your computer, use the mouse. Place the cursor (arrow) over the image you want, right click (click the right-hand mouse button) the picture or image you want to copy and select 'Copy' from the menu that appears. Return to the IWB software and click on the 'Paste' icon, or click on the page where you would like it to be pasted, and press CTRL and the V key at the same time. Both options will paste the image onto your flipchart page.

A word of warning

If you are using sounds, video clips or images that you have found on the Internet, make sure that any copyright associated with them is not infringed. There are a number of websites listed in the resources section at the back of the book that contain copyright-free materials. In some cases, a credit to the photographer is required; in others you are free to use the photographs without conditions. It is important that you teach this aspect of copyright law to the children. Even though it is possible to copy images from websites, it is not always legal to do so.

A bonus is that some IWBs have a record function that enables you to replay the stages you have gone through to arrive at an end result. This is a great way to recap for the children before they work independently and to reinforce expected models of working.

There is further information on using flipcharts in the chapters on the curriculum, and a photocopiable list of websites that provide free downloadable flipcharts can be found on pages 54–58.

Interactivity

Once you feel as confident using the IWB as you would a traditional board, it is time to develop a more interactive relationship with it. To begin, the IWB is great for displaying text and images in much the same way as an OHP. Text can be typed in, copied and pasted from sources such as the Internet – or scanned if a scanner with appropriate software is linked to your computer. The text can be presented to the children in much the same way as a big book is used in a literacy lesson.

"What's wrong with the font size?"

Remember that the font size needs to be clear – approximately 18–20 pt. A sans-serif font usually works best. Do not use too much emboldening or italicising. Aim to fit text onto one page so that you don't need to scroll up or down. Pressing F11 on your keyboard will make an Internet page appear larger on screen, removing the top toolbar. Press F11 again to restore. If you lose your lower toolbar, pressing CTRL and Esc will usually restore it. You can customise your toolbars, making them simpler for children to use, by removing tools not needed for the current activity. Increasing the font size of an Internet page can often be done by going to 'View', selecting 'Text size' and then selecting 'Larger'.

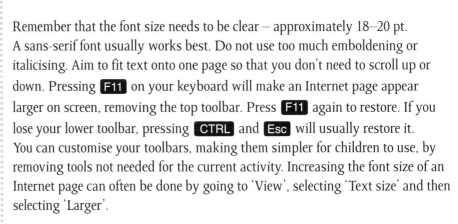

Tip: copying and pasting text

Highlight the text you want to copy by placing the cursor (arrow) before it, holding down the left mouse button and dragging a tinted bar along to highlight the text, then right click on the text and select 'Copy' (or hold down the CTRL key and press the C key once on your keyboard), open the program that you want to use the text in, right click on the screen and select 'Paste' (or hold down the CTRL key and press the V key once) to paste it into that application.

Tip: scanning software

Scanners often have Optical Character Recognition (OCR) software included. This program enables the computer to recognise letters and words from a piece of scanned text. It means you can work with the text, amending and annotating it using your word-processing and/or IWB software, rather than simply having a picture of the text that you cannot interact with, which is what a standard scan would produce.

Once the text is on the IWB, the IWB pens can be used in the same way that an OHP pen can be, so the text can be underlined, highlighted, circled, crossed out, improved and so on, introducing the 'I' of IWB – interactive.

Have a go

Copy and paste some text from the Internet or from a word-processed file already on your computer onto a flipchart page on your IWB. Try using the IWB pens to highlight, underline, circle and so on.

Think about these things:

- What line width is best for underlining?
- What colours will the children be able to see clearly?
- Are all of the highlighter colours easy to read through?
- When you use text, does it need to be enlarged or spaced out more?

There are plenty of other ways to use the IWB in an interactive way. These will be covered later. Here are some basic ideas.

Using images:

- Developing independent lines of enquiry.
- Starting points for shared writing.
- Starting points for independent writing.
- Developing numeracy skills.
- Using video clips to demonstrate points in lessons such as PE.
- Using video clips as a starting point for children's work in many subjects.

Using sound:

- Create moods, enhance images or set the tone/style of writing.
- Record the children and use the file within a presentation.

Presenting

Assessment for learning is now part of teaching and learning. The IWB is perfect for offering the children the opportunity to self- or peer-assess their efforts. It is very easy to present the children's work on the IWB. Written work can be quickly scanned in and used during a plenary session to highlight examples of good practice, or to correct common misconceptions, and digital stills and video cameras can be used to record and review children's performance across the curriculum. This will be covered in later chapters.

Diary

Notes from the front line – the class teacher

Back from the Christmas hols already and it doesn't even seem I left! The room looks neat and tidy – Di's done a lovely job, as always. Shame I forgot to water the plants, though.

What a day! Having a student teacher in the class last term really stopped me from getting on with familiarising myself with the interactive whiteboard. Sometimes I think if you looked up 'technophobe' in the dictionary you'd see a picture of me!

Had the caretaker do some furniture moving over the holiday and at least now the laptop is in a place where I can see it without standing on a ladder. Those cables are a bit of a nightmare, though – how am I supposed to know which one goes in which socket when they are all black and look identical? Must ask the technician to get them clipped together and out of sight.

Finally managed to get the laptop set up and working before the children came in (even remembered to plug the speaker cable in this time – must be getting better) but then found out that I couldn't access the network. Great start to the new year!

Chapter 3 Enhancing your interactive whiteboard practice

The positive impact of interactivity

One of the main problems I found when I first started using an IWB was that my lesson timing went to pieces. I would find myself rushing the children to get their work finished so that we could fit in a plenary.

As a result of receiving feedback from my head teacher, who had been observing a lesson, I realised where the problem lay. I was trying to cram too much in – I was so excited by the IWB that I felt that I had to share it with my class.

"With so many wives, how did you have time to do any kinging?"

IWBs are exciting. They enable us to do things we would never have dreamt of doing before. For example, when was the last time your OHP enabled your class to interview an interactive Henry VIII during a literacy lesson? However – and this is crucial – they are not able to teach for us. An IWB cannot make a poor lesson good. It can, in the right hands, make a good lesson even better.

You should always bear in mind that you are the skilled professional in the classroom. You need to use your professional judgement about when the IWB should be used interactively, when it should be used as a traditional whiteboard and when it should not be used at all. In this chapter I aim to draw out some key considerations and recent research to help you to develop and feel confident about this aspect of your classroom practice.

Contribution to teaching and learning

In 2002 the Office of Standards in Education (Ofsted) reported on the use of ICT in primary schools, noting that:

> interactive whiteboards . . . are capable of enhancing the quality of both teaching and learning, for example in introducing topics of shape and space in mathematics and in the manipulation of letters, words and texts in literacy hours. It is often pupils' use of these whiteboards that enlivens a lesson.
>
> HMI, *Information and Communication Technology in Primary Schools* (2002)

Without a doubt, this continues to apply. Over the past few years, I have seen marked improvements in the motivation, concentration and quality of discussions of the children I have taught. Even the most reticent want to participate. With some of these children this is something that no amount of cajoling has been able to achieve before.

Case Study

Case study 1: Play scripts

I had been using an IWB for a few weeks before I really noticed the effect it was having on my class. To start with, the children seemed to be gaining more from the introductions I gave to activities. I was using the elements that I considered were good practice before: discussions with partners, thinking time, shared planning, modelled writing and so on. However, the children seemed to be more focused during this part of the lesson.

When we began work on writing play scripts, as an introduction I used the IWB to show a film trailer I had downloaded from a website called Jurassic Punk. I chose the trailer of *The Cat in the Hat* as I thought the children might respond well to it. Before the lesson, I used the IWB software to prepare a description of a section of the trailer as though from a book. I made sure that there were examples of speech in speech marks, a range of dialogue verbs and descriptions of actions.

To start the lesson, we read the text I had prepared, and then watched the trailer up to a point where I had decided to stop. After this, we discussed how the text related to the trailer and agreed that the text would have been no use for the actors to learn their lines from. The children re-read the text with a partner and in their pairs wrote down on their mini dry-wipe boards examples of speech that they could see. I selected some children to highlight examples they had found at the IWB, using the IWB pen and software to make them stand out.

www.jurassicpunk.com

From there, we quickly cut and pasted the highlighted words (including speech marks) onto the next page of the interactive flipchart that I had titled 'The Cat in the Hat – the play script'. After reading the heading, we briefly discussed what we would expect in a play script, which enabled me to assess broadly their knowledge from the previous school year. We then began to organise the copied text. After some thinking time in their pairs, I asked children to come out to the IWB. We began to develop the text by removing the speech marks, aligning it appropriately, writing character names in the margin, adding stage directions, adding a short sentence setting the scene at the start of the script and so on. After a couple of lesson introductions, we had a play script that the whole class had helped to compile through traditional methods and new ones.

The IWB made the whole process easy. We moved backwards and forwards through pages on the flipchart, and at the end of each lesson I saved the work quickly, ready to review the following day to refresh the children's memories and continue with the next stage.

The most motivational element of the whole week's work was that the children would not see the whole trailer at the end of Friday's lesson unless they worked really hard through the week. They all did, and we all enjoyed the reward immensely.

This case study illustrates Ofsted's comments. The IWB was used in ways that enhanced the teaching and learning. Watching the trailer gave the children a chance to relate their work to another medium. The IWB was used in tandem with traditional teaching methods and supported the teaching and learning taking place.

My teaching has been enhanced in many ways by using an IWB. I am able to be more creative in the resources that I use as I can find many things on the Internet to share with the children that I did not have access to before.

The benefits of interactivity

I have seen an increase in the concentration, focus and enjoyment of the children I have taught using an IWB.

One of the greatest benefits is the ease with which I can recall a document saved from a previous lesson, displaying it to refresh the children's memories, or to revise previous thoughts and hypotheses. The simple act of saying 'I'll just save what we've done now' gives the work validity and importance. I do this sometimes even if we are unlikely to come back to the work again. At the end of a week, I review the documents I have saved during the week and delete anything I know that I am not going to come back to.

A message praising IWBs placed on an Internet forum quickly received a great many responses, some of which are listed below.

- You can prepare most of your board work in advance. This means that you don't have to have your back to the class for more than a second.
- Your resources are ready year after year, lesson after lesson.
- You can use images, colours and graphics to assist visual learners, and sound to help auditory learners.

My first IWB was set up in a corner of my classroom that was visible to another class in the same year. During the introduction to one literacy lesson, I realised that children from the other class were leaning back on their chairs and watching the IWB, even though I was delivering the same lesson as their teacher. Having my materials displayed in colour on a large screen with a little bit of animation and music made them more appealing to the children. Soon children from other classes were asking me when they would get an IWB so that they didn't have to look at the OHP any more.

Case Study

Case study 2: Creating calm

One year I had a particularly challenging Year 6 class. I bought a book of meditations for children called *Relax Kids*. Each day after lunch I played a calm piece of music through the IWB, displayed an image of a peaceful landscape, and read a meditation. It worked really well. I used this again at the start of each day in the build-up to SATs. In time, I developed my own meditations to offer the children encouragement and opportunities to find a quiet space inside themselves. This worked so well that the children began to ask when they came into class if we were doing a meditation.

Relax Kids: Aladdin's Magic Carpet, Marneta Viegas, O Books, 2004.

There is an excellent resource called Thinking Out of the Box, which I have adapted for use with an IWB. I select an activity and type it up for use on the IWB at the start of the morning. An example is writing down a noun for each letter of their name to describe themselves. This is a more creative way to get children focused than going over what happened in the playground or before they arrived at school.

Have a go

Here is a simple creative activity for the start of a day. Prepare a flipchart on the IWB. Have a look through your CDs, at school or at home, and find a calming track.

On your flipchart page create a table with three columns. Label them as shown below; you could put a few examples in each column:

Colours	Verbs	Feelings

When the children come in, ask them to listen to the music and think of words to go in each of the columns while you are taking the register. After the register has been taken, discuss the words they thought of, inviting some of them to write their words on the IWB.

Later in the day, or maybe the following day, use a piece of music with a different mood – perhaps something dramatic, energetic or eerie – and repeat the exercise. Refer back to the table you saved previously to discuss the differences.

Benefits to children and learning

We recognise that children learn best when they are involved in an activity that is relevant to them and enjoyable. There are few children who don't like television, and to many the IWB first appears to be a huge television screen. The best thing about this particular screen is that they have a significant input. What you put on the IWB stands a good chance of being focused on and thought about if you are tapping into the concerns and interests of the children in front of it.

Case studies 1 and 2 show how the IWB captures and retains the children's attention. An IWB is a major motivating factor for many children. Those of you with pupils who show little interest in school work will find it especially effective.

An IWB reinforces learning through the use of images and pictures, supporting the visual learner. By organising such information using a pen, pointer or finger, children are enhancing their learning. This consolidates the teaching points being explored and is great for kinaesthetic learners too.

The use of an IWB can add an element of fun to teaching and learning. A sense of enjoyment is an important aspect of learning. The IWB's ability to integrate animation, sound, video and text provides support for a range of learning styles.

The use of an IWB in conjunction with smaller, individual dry-wipe boards in pairs offers children opportunities for increased communication and collaboration, as seen in Case study 1.

Access to the Internet, software resources and clipart all enhance your teaching. By incorporating many stimuli to get our teaching points across, we are able to target all the children in our class. Research into individual learning styles supports the use of an IWB in this way.

Benefits to children with special educational needs

I have been involved in an IWB pilot project that included teachers from across an LEA. One teacher came from a special needs school, and he shared with us by anecdote and video footage his experience of using an IWB. The IWB was a resource that enabled the children in his class to participate in the lessons, interacting with him, the resources and each other in ways that had not been possible before. They could use the SMART Board easily as they had an extendable pointer to interact with it. They used the board in numeracy to compare shapes and sizes of objects, dragging them and reordering them according to certain criteria. Counting and number work was made possible by the highly visible resources on the IWB. Children who had never participated in lessons before, or even looked at the teacher for extended periods of time, were starting to take active roles in the lesson. They were willing to come up to the board and complete work while communicating with the teacher.

www.inclusive.co.uk

Children who were unable to move to the board could control it using a wireless *switch*. This was made possible because the IWB was connected to a computer that used a wide range of switch software. The children could work and interact with the IWB in a way that suited them. A wide range of programs that can be controlled by switches have been specially designed for pupils with special educational needs. Try the website in the margin to get you started.

Switch. A tool that enables children with motor-control difficulties to use a computer by selecting items or options on screen by pressing a large button rather than manipulating a mouse. A slate/tablet PC or a wireless mouse also enables children to control the IWB from their seat.

Having a consistent screen layout will help many pupils. They will begin to associate specific events with icons in a particular place.

The IWB offers practice in motor skills by dragging and dropping, as well as being usable by children who find conventional mouse control difficult. An IWB therefore offers children with specific needs or disabilities the opportunity to overcome a number of barriers to learning. At the simplest level, visual patterns and tracking activities can be created very easily by using, for example, the free Windows Media Player. Digital video and stills cameras can be used by the children to record work, and the results can be viewed by everyone. This lets some children share their thoughts, opinions and ideas more effectively than is usually possible.

Preparing to use the interactive whiteboard

Thorough planning is as vital when using an IWB as it is when teaching without one. It is all too easy to go off at a tangent, playing rather than interacting.

Overall development in school needs to be led by the senior management team, and interactivity is no different. The best way to develop interactivity is to put aside time in staff meetings or INSET days for everyone to get involved. Making this part of the whole-school development plan is fundamental for success. Follow-up sessions need to be held to develop planning to incorporate ICT use and to share good practice across year groups. The best training comes from sessions where staff learn from each other in a relaxed atmosphere.

Upload. To transfer (data or programs), usually from a peripheral computer or device, to a central computer.

Simply put, uploading is sending something from your computer to someone else's.

Having said this, there is nothing to stop you from developing your own materials and finding your own resources. Make full use of the Internet. There are plenty of websites to help you resource your lessons, many of them offering the facility to download resources onto your computer for your own use. Some even let you *upload* your work; why not share what you are doing with others?

Have a go!

Think about your plans for the forthcoming weeks. Consider how the IWB could be integrated into them. Later chapters will provide detailed guidance. Begin by making small changes.

Possible starting points could be as follows:

- Sentence-level work looking at specific features of a shared text.
- Brainstorming existing knowledge on a specific topic to review later.
- Displaying pictures as an introduction to a lesson or new topic.
- Displaying pictures as a prompt or stimulus for writing.
- Using the free Interactive Teaching Programs (ITPs) to teach a mental and oral starter in numeracy (see page 62).
- Use clipart/images/shapes from the IWB software to initiate discussion.

Set a target of using the IWB interactively in at least one literacy and one numeracy lesson a week to begin with. As your confidence grows, increase the number of interactive uses you plan and the range of subjects you cover.

How to start

In order to use an IWB interactively, you need to be prepared. Organise and manage your files so that you can keep track of the material you create and use regularly. Do this by creating a range of folders on the computer linked to your IWB or on your school's network. There are a number of ways to do this in Windows. Below is one way:

① Open the folder on your computer that you want to create a new folder in. I suggest that you use your 'My Documents' folder.

② Right click using the right-hand button of the mouse on any of the white space within the window that opens.

③ Select 'New' from the menu and then select 'Folder' from the menu that appears. A new folder appears.

④ Type the name of the folder in the highlighted box beneath it.

⑤ Press 'Enter' or click on any white space to save the name of the folder.

If you are using Windows XP, you can do this as explained below:

① Open the folder on your computer that you want to create a new folder in. I suggest that you use your 'My Documents' folder.
② Left click with your mouse on 'Make a new folder' in the File and Folder tasks column on the left-hand side. A new folder appears.
③ Type the name of the folder in the highlighted box beneath it.
④ Press 'Enter' or click on any white space to save the name of the folder.

If the 'Make a new folder' option is not shown, ensure that nothing has been selected in the window that has opened. Simply left click using the left-hand button of the mouse anywhere on the white space in the window.

"If only my filing cabinets were as tidy as my on-screen folders."

You can repeat this procedure as many times as you like, and you may find that you need to create folders within folders in order to subdivide the contents. I organise my curriculum resources into three termly folders. In each term I subdivide the materials into subject folders. I further subdivide the subjects into weekly folders. Finally, I follow a set procedure for naming any materials. For example:

Day 1 – story setting
Day 2 – character profiles
Day 3 – speech marks.

In this way, I can find all my resources quickly and easily.

The interactive whiteboard's place in a lesson

The IWB can be used at various stages of the lesson. It can serve as a means to introduce the aim of a lesson and present introductory materials. It will help you to maintain a sense of pace during this part of the lesson. You may have to build in some thinking time for the children to look and process the new information displayed before continuing with the introduction. Try to keep your questions open, and remember that the good questioning skills you used before having your IWB are just as crucial now.

After the introduction, the children can work through examples on the IWB to consolidate the teaching points. These need to be thought through so that they are truly interactive and informative. This phase can provide working examples that the children can refer to when they work away from the IWB. Alternatively, the IWB could be switched off, and referred to at a later point in the lesson.

The IWB can be used effectively during a plenary. Amongst the things that you could do are working through earlier examples again, playing a game to reiterate the teaching point and reviewing some scanned work from a child.

There are so many benefits in using an IWB that it will become an integral part of your teaching.

Conclusion

There are so many benefits in using an IWB that it will become an integral part of your teaching. However, remember that the use of an IWB should not be to the detriment of other teaching tools. It is only one of many tools that you have at your disposal. We must constantly exercise our professional judgement and use what is most appropriate for the task.

In addition, we must not forget the importance of:

- placing lessons in appropriate contexts;
- linking learning objectives to prior learning;
- using a variety of resources to explain and clarify learning intentions;
- drama and role play;
- differentiation;
- mixed-ability groupings;
- discussions;
- independent research and enquiry;
- quality formative and summative assessment.

All of these are vital elements of a teacher's toolkit. The IWB can be used to aid and facilitate them.

We have come a long way from the old 'chalk and talk' methods of teaching, but if we aren't careful it is easy to fall back into that style with an IWB.

There is nothing to be learnt from watching a teacher demonstrate what a whiz they are on the IWB while the children sit with eyes glazed over. That's what children may do with normal televisions. Remember that your children can have starring roles with this screen.

The interactions we generate using an IWB must, above all else, be meaningful for the teacher and learner. They must aid these and they must involve the children. In the next four chapters I aim to show you ways in which you can achieve this in literacy, numeracy, science and the foundation subjects.

Before this, read the next diary entry on page 28.

Diary

Notes from the front line – the class teacher

What a day! One or two successes and a lot of stress!

I spent some of last night marking and then preparing the resources for today's literacy lesson, and was really looking forward to getting started. I got into school and set up the laptop with no problems. That's progress for you.

I had typed up the date and the morning's aims on the flipchart, and even added a picture of a sun to brighten up the board. I opened the folder to find this work and then it all went to pieces.

I know I saved the work when I shut down the computer last night. 'Do you want to save the changes you have made?' What would we do without those reminders? I certainly did. I'm sure I did.

But when I opened the folder, the work wasn't there! I looked everywhere in the 'My Documents' folder for it. There were a load of files in there and I wish I knew what half of them were. The other half were science, art, literacy and numeracy stuff from the autumn; my presentation on the Year 3 trip; maths pictures from last half-term – but no literacy materials for today.

I wasted half an hour looking for the work and then had five minutes left to get the rest of the morning sorted out – this ICT business drives me mad sometimes. I know that it will make it easier next year, but right now that's not helping. I hate getting so stressed before the kids come in.

Chapter 4
Literacy

The ideas in this chapter are divided into two sections:

- short games and activities;
- resourcing and supporting lessons.

Some activities could fit into either of the sections. I have tried to place the more interactive ideas in the first one. The suggestions in the second section will enable interactivity, but may require greater teacher input. Beginning on page 54, there is a photocopiable list of websites that offer support and resources, both free and for purchase, in this area and others.

Short games and activities

Handwriting grids

A page from a handwriting book can be scanned and used as a background on a flipchart page on your IWB. Some IWBs have appropriate background sheets in their resource banks.

Handwriting grids can be used to demonstrate how letters/words should be formed using an IWB pen and the IWB's handwriting-recognition software. Children can be asked to demonstrate letters and words as part of the consolidation and plenary phases of a lesson. The IWB could be left on during the independent part of a lesson to demonstrate the correct formation of the letters for the children.

Spelling activities

1. Look, say, cover, write, check

There are interactive look, say, cover, write, check programs available to download from the Internet if you use this system to practise spellings. This activity could be used with small groups of children. You can easily create a simple look, say, cover, write, check activity using your IWB's software.

www.bbc.co.uk/skillswise/words/spelling

Have a go

Write or type the words you are referring to on the IWB and use a coloured shape to cover each of them. It is easy to slide the shape off a word using an IWB stylus or a finger. This allows the word to be shown, and covered again while the children write it down on their mini dry-wipe boards. The word can then be revealed to check against.

2. Spelling patterns

Spelling patterns can be practised and rehearsed very effectively using an IWB. Make flipchart pages with various images placed on them that demonstrate the same spelling rule: C–V–C words, sh- and ch- beginnings, -ight endings, -s or -es endings for plurals and so on.

You can find such images on most IWBs' clipart software or the Internet. Once you have gathered the images you need, type the associated words on the relevant flipchart page. You could break the words down into their component parts. The page can be created in a very simple way, with parts of words typed under each of the images and various letters that can be used to complete the words in a letter bank in the form of a rectangle at the bottom of the screen. The children can select and drag the correct components to the correct picture.

www.clipart4schools.com

"Now you see it.
Now you don't."

3. Word prediction

Similarly to the look, say, cover, write, check activity, word prediction can be practised by typing a selection of words onto a flipchart page. A shape can be used to cover a word. This shape can be moved, revealing one letter of the word at a time, allowing the children to predict or guess the word from the clues they have. You can develop discussion points about effective spelling strategies from this simple activity.

4. Anagrams

Spellings can be practised in spelling group sessions at appropriate moments by setting up a flipchart with one example of the week's spellings on a page. The letters of the word should be typed up individually so that they can be moved around the IWB independently of the others. Rearrange the letters to produce an anagram.

I have used this activity in a class for which I produced three spelling lists, one for each of the three ability levels. I divided a flipchart page into three sections and typed each group's spellings as anagrams in a different colour. The children soon became used to their group's colour and enjoyed the challenge of trying to solve their group's words first.

Children can work in pairs, groups or individually, depending on age and ability, to solve the anagram. There are many ways for the children to record their answers: mini dry-wipe boards, putting up their hand when they have solved the anagram and so on. The first child or group to get the correct answer could rearrange the letters on the IWB to show it.

5. Sentence construction

This is an excellent mental starter for literacy, using one of Pie Corbett's ideas. Write or type a simple sentence on the IWB; for example, 'The boy ate his red lolly hungrily.' Under the sentence write a series of six numbered instructions. For example:

① Change a noun.
② Change/add an adjective.
③ Change a verb.
④ Change/add an adverb.
⑤ Change/add a phrase or clause.
⑥ Change the position of a phrase or clause.

The last two points are for older children. If you are working with younger children, the last two points could be repeats of earlier instructions.

The majority of IWBs have an interactive dice tool that will roll a die on screen when instructed to do so. Promethean and SMART Board (Smart Notebook V.9) both have interactive die. They can be also be downloaded from the Easiteach website. Use your interactive die to generate a number that the children use to guide them to the correct option from the list. The children, individually or in pairs, adapt the sentence in response to the option chosen. They could write their version on their own mini dry-wipe board. After an allotted time, you could ask volunteers to share their new sentences with the rest of the group, inviting them to record their work on the IWB.

www.smarttech.com
www.smart-uk.co.uk
www.easiteach.co.uk

Resourcing and supporting lessons

Working with texts

1. Word prediction

Predicting words in texts is an important aspect of encouraging children to use more mature language. Copying and pasting text into the IWB's software is quick and easy. You may wish to type short extracts from an appropriate big book or story you use as part of your literacy work instead. Certain words in the extract can be hidden by shapes or drawn over with an IWB pen set to the same colour as the screen background. The children can explore the amended passage and predict what word has been hidden by writing their choice on a mini dry-wipe board. You can discuss their choices before asking a child to reveal the hidden word. The first time a word is 'magically' revealed is highly effective.

Some whiteboard software enables you to put a spotlight over a chosen area of the IWB. Others have a reveal tool that allows you to show a small part of the board at a time. These tools are useful to highlight and reveal parts of words. They also have many other applications.

2. Reordering texts

Reordering a text enables children to show their understanding of the appropriate features of a certain style of writing. You could type various parts of a text, such as a letter, onto a flipchart page and present them on the IWB in the wrong order. The children can discuss as a group or with a partner how to reorder the text, making notes to refer to as they go. Then some can come to the IWB to highlight, *drag and drop* parts of the text in order to arrange the passage correctly.

Drag and drop. Clicking on an object such as a piece of clipart or a file in a folder by holding down the left-hand mouse button with the cursor over the item you wish to move, and moving the mouse to drag it into the desired place on the screen before releasing the mouse button to drop it in the new place.

Asking children to sequence the parts of a story or a set of instructions provides a purposeful way for the children to demonstrate their understanding and awareness of the work.

3. Creating settings

Most IWB software has the facility to place background scenes on a flipchart page. These cannot be moved or altered, so you can drag and drop other images onto them and create a setting for a story, play, description, recount and so on.

With the Promethean software, you can set the size of the flipchart page on the IWB (the white area on the board) as a percentage of its true size. You can then drag and drop clipart onto the space around the page. Children can choose from these images, dragging and dropping them onto the paper to create a setting of their own making. Once complete, the page can be returned to its full size and any clipart that has not been selected will be covered, allowing the children to focus on their new setting. Such settings can be used as a basis for exploring key components of story writing, to stimulate vibrant story beginnings, and to look at how to build atmosphere and detail into a story.

4. Annotating images and pictures

You can scan an image to display on an IWB, and use the IWB's pens and other on-screen tools, such as shapes and highlighters, to annotate it. An IWB's software usually contains a 'photo' option that enables you to capture anything on the screen so that it can be recorded on a flipchart page. This image can be annotated and any relevant notes or vocabulary can be recorded in the space around it. Work can be saved and used in later lessons when needed. This could be a child's sketch, a photograph you have taken, or even a scanned image of a collection of autumn leaves to use as a basis for poetry writing or artwork.

Another way to use images is to scan or take a digital photograph of part of an object. This helps to focus the children's attention on a specific area. Using the IWB's 'photo' function again, the chosen area can be saved onto a flipchart page and enlarged for the children to annotate or to work with in some other way.

Case study 3: pictures and images

In one literacy lesson on story settings, I displayed a picture of a Tudor kitchen and asked the children to work with their discussion partners to pick out aspects that they felt needed elaboration. I asked some children to come to the IWB to annotate the picture in the ways we discussed. After completing this task, I printed the flipchart page for each child to stick in their book, creating a resource to support their independent work.

In another lesson on action and suspense paragraphs, I annotated a scanned line drawing of a cave system to help the children to organise their writing into paragraphs. I used various images and clipart, copied from the Internet, to develop a list of verbs with the children to use in their writing. I saved the work and we were able to revisit it every morning before moving on to the next stage of the story.

5. Annotating children's work

As mentioned in Chapter 1, scanners are extremely useful in conjunction with an IWB. When nearing a plenary, I often scan examples of the children's work that demonstrate the successful – or, better still, the not-so-successful – application of the lesson's aims. To do this appropriately, it is important to establish an ethos in which children feel proud to have their work shown on the

Unlocking Formative Assessment: Practical Strategies for Enhancing Pupils' Learning in the Primary Classroom
Shirley Clarke, Hodder Arnold, 2001

IWB. I stress that we look at each other's work to highlight to the rest of the class what each child has achieved before looking to see how they can improve their writing. This is a good way to integrate assessment for learning into your practice and an effective motivator for the children.

6. Taking pictures using digital cameras

I have seen lessons in which children have gone off in small groups, each group with a digital camera, to photograph areas within the school or class. They have used a computer to collate these photographs, add captions and save their work. This work has been presented to the rest of the class in a plenary or as part of subsequent lessons using the IWB. Taking pictures enables the children to have ownership of the learning and to develop their learning as they want, within the boundaries you have set. This sort of work can be used to develop speaking and listening skills, presentation skills and writing for a specific purpose.

"Make sure you get its best side."

7. Big books

You can purchase published electronic big books for your IWB from any mainstream educational publisher. However, it is very easy to download some or to make your own. Making your own obviously takes longer initially, but some of the construction stages can be completed by children as part of a lesson or you can do this yourself in an introduction to a lesson. Many useful teaching points can be explored in this manner.

Kent LEA's website has some big book materials for Key Stage 1. The MAPE website has a downloadable program that allows you or your children to use your own digital images to make a big book. Alternatively, you can create your own big books or e-stories for your IWB using the board's software, PowerPoint, Softease Presenter or any other similar presentation program. It is possible to incorporate images and text, and to record yourself reading the text using a microphone and the sound recorder that comes with Windows (find this on your computer by following the directions in the margin). Version 2 of Promethean's ActivBoard software also has a sound recording facility. The spoken text you create can be used alongside the text on screen so that the activity becomes much more than a reading exercise.

www.kented.org.uk/ngfl
www.mape.org.uk

Another version of the e-story is an interactive story. These can be created relatively easily using a presentation program such as PowerPoint. The first page you create gives the initial sentence, such as 'It is dark and you hear some scratching from inside your wardrobe.' At the bottom of this page the children can be offered two options such as these:

Windows Sound Recorder

Click on Start → Programs → Accessories → Entertainment → Sound Recorder

- Do you turn over in bed and try to go back to sleep?
- Do you investigate the scratching?

These two options can be set up to link to other slides in the presentation, which the children will be sent to, depending on the option they choose. The story can progress in the same manner. The text on each slide can be supplemented by images and include a spoken reading.

A word of warning

This is something to be tackled once you feel comfortable using the software, as it can be very labour intensive. If you don't think you are ready to try this yet, don't worry. You can come back to it at a later stage.

Case Study

Case Study 4: e-story

I have scanned the text of a passage that I had previously had on an OHT into PowerPoint and read it with a whole class. The level of interest and enthusiasm rose dramatically with the introduction of the e-story. I recorded myself reading the text and asked the children to read parts of it along with me. They all appeared to be concentrating on the passage on the board, and without exception were able to join in when asked. This had not happened in previous lessons using the same passage on an OHT. I believe that this increase in enthusiasm was largely due to the fact that children like to be read to. Combining this with ICT meant that they were enthused and remained focused. The quality of work that came out of the independent part of the lesson reflected their enthusiasm and focus.

Have a go

Prepare a flipchart or presentation to use in a literacy lesson. Scan the text you decide to use into the IWB software or a presentation package such as PowerPoint. Different scanners operate in different ways, but typically they have a 'quick-scan' button on the top or front of the scanner that will automatically open the scanning software and begin the scanning process. With some scanners you may need to open the software manually to scan the image you wish to use.

Remember that often when scanning text, unless you choose 'Scan as text' from the options, the software will treat the text like a picture and you will be unable to alter individual words in the text on the IWB.

Now you have your text in place, find some clipart to illustrate the key events of that page if there are no illustrations already. This can help children later when recalling the text.

If you are feeling brave, use the sound recorder and a microphone to record your voice and add it to your presentation.

Using the Windows Sound Recorder

① Plug a microphone into the appropriate socket of your computer.
② Open the sound recorder.
③ Click on the Record icon with the left-hand mouse button.
④ Start speaking.
⑤ Click on the Stop icon when you have finished speaking.
⑥ Click on 'File'.
⑦ Click on 'Save'.
⑧ Save the sound file in an appropriate location in your 'My Documents' folder ready to use in your presentation.

Adding the sounds you created in PowerPoint

① Open the PowerPoint presentation you created.
② Click on 'Insert' with the left-hand mouse button.
③ Click on 'Movies and Sounds'.
④ Click on 'Sound from File'.
⑤ Locate and select the sound file you created with the sound recorder.
⑥ Click on 'OK'.
⑦ A small speaker icon will appear on the PowerPoint slide.

The sound file can be set up to play as soon as the slide has loaded, and can also be dragged off the slide onto the area around it so that it is not visible when playing the presentation.

If you have created a number of PowerPoint pages for your passage, create a separate sound file for each page.

8. Using video clips

Video clips and film trailers can be freely downloaded from the Internet. One site is Jurassic Punk. Using such resources offers an excellent opportunity to grab the children's attention with something up to date and relevant.

www.jurassicpunk.com

You can use these materials in many ways, depending on the style and content of the trailer. Here are some examples of their use for writing activities:

- playscripts;
- newspaper reports;
- instructions;
- recounts;
- continuing the story;
- diaries;
- leaflets;
- letters;
- persuasive writing.

It is possible to use a film trailer in many ways. The IWB allows you to pause the video at a specific point, and to copy the image into the board's flipchart if you want to.

9. Sounds and music

Using sounds and music is a great way to set the mood. You can do this without a computer or IWB – all you need is a CD player and a CD. However, it is possible, using a computer and an IWB, to utilise sounds and music that are individual and not on a CD.

www.napster.co.uk
www.apple.com
www.findsounds.com

A word of warning

Once again, there are important copyright issues that need to be recognised here. Any sounds or music that you download from the Internet must be copyright free or paid for in some way. Downloading a pop song from a fan's website would be breaking copyright laws. It is possible to obtain tracks from sites such as Napster and Apple's iTunes, for which you pay a subscription or download fee. However, there are plenty of locations for downloading copyright-free sounds. On FindSounds, you can simply type in the sound you wish to hear. The website will search the Internet and return the results for you. It is possible to listen to and download the sounds for your own use.

Case Study

Case study 5: Setting a scene

Using FindSounds, I downloaded sound effects to support a writing week using Van Gogh's *Pavement Café*, including a horse and cart, people talking, the sounds of glasses and cutlery, and some accordion music. I used a program called Audacity to compile these sounds into a two-minute soundtrack to set the scene. I decided to play some music during the writing time, and found pieces of French accordion music. The children enjoyed the work and responded well to the activities, producing some excellent work.

www.sourceforge.net/projects/audacity

A word of warning

This is another of those activities that, whilst rewarding and worthwhile, can take a lot of time. Perhaps you could try this out for a special themed week that you are planning. That gives you plenty of time to prepare and builds a sense of anticipation in the children.

10. Internet links (hyperlinks)

Supporting children's learning with links to the Internet is an excellent way to place the learning into context. I have seen web links used to great effect in Key Stage 1 classrooms when the children have been developing research skills. The teacher had set up the flipchart pages to support the children with the structure and style of report writing, and as the week progressed they mind mapped the chosen topic – in this case dinosaurs – wrote a shared introduction to the piece on the IWB, and went online to research the topic and find images to support their writing. From there, they produced their own independent writing.

Another such lesson used digital photographs taken of and by the children over the course of a day's activities on the Chinese New Year, which included Chinese writing, watching a dragon dance, and wearing traditional clothing. The children talked in pairs about what they had done during the day, and wrote useful connectives and opening phrases on individual dry-wipe boards. These were collated and presented on the IWB for use later in the lesson. The children referred back to this work and to the photographs while working independently.

Setting up links to the Internet is possible using most IWB software. If you find that you are unable to do it, consider using PowerPoint, Word or Textease as an alternative.

Creating hyperlinks in PowerPoint and Word

① Log on to the Internet and find the website that you require. Highlight the address by left clicking on it. Right click and select 'copy' to copy the website address from the Address box at the top of Internet Explorer.
② Open PowerPoint or Word if it is not already open.
③ Place some clipart on a fresh page, and, if you are using Windows XP, right click on it and select 'Hyperlink'.
④ If you are using another Windows version, click on 'Insert' and select 'Hyperlink'.
⑤ Left click in the panel beside 'Address'.
⑥ Press CTRL and V to paste the copied website address into this panel.
⑦ Click on 'OK'.
⑧ When the presentation is running, you will be able to select the clipart to link to the appropriate web page.

If you want to create a hyperlink without using clipart, then omit instruction 3 from the list.

Creating hyperlinks in Textease

① Copy the website address from Internet Explorer as above.
② Open Textease if it is not already open.
③ Place some clipart or text on the page and select it by left clicking if it is clipart or highlighting if it is text.
④ Click on the 'Links' icon (the one that looks like a chain).
⑤ Right-click in the space beside 'Address' and select 'Paste'.
⑥ Ensure that there are ticks in all of the boxes in the window (click in them if there aren't).
⑦ Click on the X to close the 'Links' window.
⑧ Clicking on the text or clipart will link to the appropriate web page.

Diary

Notes from the front line – the class teacher

I really enjoyed watching John teach his literacy lesson today – it has given me a huge amount to think about. I think I've got a long way to go before I am going to be as quick as he was with the board, but at least I know that I can go and ask him for help if I need it.

I'd never thought that it would be so easy to get a video clip off the Internet. Come to think of it, I never realised you could get video clips on the Internet! And the way the children responded to his questions was brilliant – it was a definite motivator for them. I think I'll try to work something similar into our year group's newspaper-writing week after half-term. Hopefully it will stop the children from saying 'I can't think of anything to write about.'

Now, how am I going to use the board tomorrow? I finally feel I'm catching up with people now!

Chapter 5
Numeracy

Maths tends to be a subject that a lot of people worry about presenting as it can be difficult to teach the abstract concepts that some mathematical understanding is based on. Numeracy lessons are probably the easiest ones to support using an IWB, for a number of reasons:

① It is possible to offer visual alternatives for the numbers, strategies and methods that we use on paper so we can teach abstract concepts in a more concrete way.
② There are plenty of resources dedicated to supporting the teaching of this subject, so we are not reliant on spending our own time preparing something we lack confidence to do.
③ There are many opportunities for the children to interact with the IWB.
④ The IWB provides an added element of interactivity to other concrete resources for this subject. It should be used to supplement these materials, not at their expense.

There is a wide range of programs and resources that can be purchased to support numeracy. Those that I have found useful include these:

- Easiteach by RM.
- Mult-e-Maths Primary Maths Software by Cambridge University Press.
- Primary Games by Mark Cogan.

www.easiteach.co.uk
www.cambridge.org
www.primarygames.co.uk

How you use these programs and the IWB is extremely important. The last thing children want to do is sit and watch you playing with the wonderful tools at your disposal, without getting the opportunity to do anything themselves to aid their learning or demonstrate their own understanding.

I have organised the tips and ideas into the following sections:

- Ways to use the IWB's tools.
- Using free resources.

Ways to use the interactive whiteboard's tools

Using shapes

1. Sorting and matching

For younger children and those with special educational needs, shapes are great for sorting and matching activities. A selection can be created beforehand to be explored and sorted in a lesson through discussion and reference to plastic shapes. Children can drag and drop the shapes into different areas of a page with headings related to their properties. They can also be asked to select, drag and drop a particular shape, identified by its properties, from a clipart gallery or previously prepared resource bank to an appropriate place on a flipchart page.

"Can we look up Mondrian on the Internet? We did him last year."

As shapes are identified in a sorting exercise, they can be moved on the IWB by the children to create a simple picture such as a house or a car.

2. Sequencing

A simple sequence can be created on a flipchart page using a range of 2-D shapes, changing their size, type or colour. These sequences can be simple or complex, depending on the age and ability of the children. Children can be asked to work on their own or with a partner to complete the sequence on a mini dry-wipe board. After an exploration of their findings, ask some children to come up and complete a sequence, choosing shapes from a prepared selection on the flipchart page. You could have part of the sequence masked by colour that is the same as the background. The children can remove the colour from the IWB using a pen to reveal if they are right.

3. Counters

It is quick and easy to create counters on your IWB. Simply find the shape or image that you want in your resource banks, decide on the fill colour if necessary, and drag it into place on a flipchart page. This object can be copied and pasted as many times as necessary and left on one side of the screen to use in the lesson. Giving children the opportunity to choose the counters to use can sometimes give the added motivation needed to grasp a concept. The ability to move counters round the screen makes mathematical concepts come alive for some children.

Counters can be used in all manner of ways. Here are a few of my ideas:

- One-to-one correspondence.
- Addition.
- Subtraction.
- Arrays for multiplication or division.
- Grouping for multiplication or division.
- Use two different types of counters to look at ratio and proportion.
- Probability.
- Logging data on a graph or pictogram.

IWB software often includes a calculator tool that could be of use for some of these activities.

4. Hiding and revealing

Elements on an IWB can easily be hidden by using a shape to mask them. Some examples follow.

Hiding numbers on a number square

One page of a flipchart could have on it a completed 100 square to support counting in tens to 100. The next page could have the same 100 square with the 10s column blanked out. Flick between the two pages as children develop an understanding of the number pattern. If a particular number is proving difficult to remember in the sequence, its masking shape can be removed to reveal it before covering it once more.

Various numbers within a certain area or number patterns could be masked to encourage children to explore the many patterns, both simple and complex, on a number square. This will help them to understand the ways in which a number square aids counting on and back in different increments.

Some IWB software allows you to create customised number squares or parts of a number square, so you do not have to type in all the numbers yourself.

Some IWB software allows you to create customised number squares or parts of a number square.

You may be able to use the 'fill' tool to mask numbers in a number square. For example, if the numbers are written in blue, set the fill colour to the same blue, then fill in the squares by placing your cursor over each of them and left clicking. If you are at the IWB, simply tap the required squares with an IWB pen or your finger. To show the numbers again, set the fill colour to the background colour of the number square and select the appropriate squares, and your numbers will appear.

Hiding numbers on a number line
The same rules of preparation apply to hiding numbers in a number line as in a number square. Numbers can be hidden to encourage counting on and back in different steps, and to explore the relationships between numbers within a pattern.

Hiding shapes
The 'Spotlight' and 'Reveal' tools are excellent for identifying shapes. Being able to reveal parts of a shape gradually or to scan a spotlight over it to highlight its attributes helps children to get to know the properties of shapes. Do this in conjunction with plastic shapes, so that children get the tactile experience too.

The children can use the IWB pens to come up and draw over the shaded area their prediction of what the shape is, and then judge their prediction as the shape is revealed.

Hiding resources or numbers that will be used later in the lesson
Having the resources that you need to hand without their being seen by the children is helpful. Create resource banks for later in a lesson and then fill the box with a masking colour. When you need them, you can remove the box to reveal the resources. Resources might include:

- numbers that are to be placed on a number line or in a number square;
- shapes or numbers that will be sorted in various ways;
- operation signs;
- answers to problems.

5. Number line activities

Many IWBs have mathematical resource banks that have prepared number lines. These are excellent time savers: some can be used straightaway and others exist as templates that just need to have numbers dropped into the grid. Once these materials exist as a flipchart page, they can be saved and used again with no preparation. They can also be amended very easily.

Programs such as Easiteach from RM and Mult-e-Maths from Cambridge University Press allow you to create customised number lines. You can set the start and end numbers, choose how many steps to be shown on the line, and decide whether the numbers are to be visible. Additionally, the numbers can be dragged from the line; they will automatically snap back into place when dropped back onto it.

The ideas below are a selection to get you thinking about how you might develop numeracy in your classroom:

- counting forwards and backwards in different steps;
- ordering numbers;
- providing aids to solving addition and subtraction problems;
- exploring the relationships between measurements.

Case Study

Case study 6: Using number lines

I used number lines recently to explore with a Year 3 class the relationship between whole numbers and tenths.

In the first lesson, I set up a flipchart with a number of pages on my IWB. On the first page I selected a blank number line with eleven check marks. I wrote the number 23 on the far left of the number line and the number 33 on the far right. I created a number bank that included all the numbers the children needed to complete the number line and some that they didn't. I asked children to discuss the sequence with a partner and encouraged some to come to the board and drag appropriate numbers from the number bank into the correct positions on the number line.

After some time, I moved on to the next page of the flipchart, where there was a number line from 0 to 10. Following some discussion about this number line, I explained that we could divide each of the sections up into even smaller sections. I revealed a number line below the 0 to 10 line that I had prepared earlier. This was marked in tenths from 0 to 1 and had lines linking the numbers to the respective numbers in the 0 to 10 number line. I explained how we had zoomed in to have a closer look at the section of the top number line between 0 and 1.

It was now possible for me to explain that, just as the section between the 0 and 1 had been divided up into 10 smaller parts, each mini-section was one tenth of the whole. I showed that this would be written as 0.1, explaining that the 0 meant that there were no whole units and that .1 represented one tenth of the whole. I then invited children to write the remaining decimals on the number line. We spent some time counting backwards and forwards in tenths between 0 and 1, using the number line as a support. Once I felt that the children were confident about the sequence, I asked them to close their eyes while I used a coloured rectangle on the IWB to cover one of the decimals. When they opened their eyes, I asked them to write on their dry-wipe boards what they thought the missing number was. I then checked their understanding by asking them to hold their boards up.

This lesson could have been done with a standard whiteboard, but the children gained much by being able to interact easily with the IWB. I appreciated the ease with which I could add, remove and cover numbers on the number line. The fact that I could prepare this all in advance was a huge time saver.

6. Angles and measurement

Most IWB software comes with an interactive ruler and protractor. The scale on the ruler can often be changed from mm and cm to inches, so metric and imperial measurements can be quickly and easily compared. If the software does not enable you to change a ruler's scale during an activity, you can normally select a second ruler with a different scale to use for comparisons. Whilst these tools do not replace your plastic versions, they are very versatile: they can be moved and rotated on the IWB as required. Some software will, if you hover the tip of an IWB pen just above the edge of the ruler or protractor, automatically draw along the edge of either tool.

These tools tend to be transparent, so not only are children able to use them to measure accurately on the IWB, but the rest of the class or group can see how they are going about the task and whether their reading is accurate – something much more difficult with a ruler or metre stick on a traditional whiteboard or using an OHP.

The ideas listed below will be a stimulus to your own thoughts and ideas for using interactive protractors and rulers.

Interactive protractors can be used to measure:

- angles drawn with a ruler;
- angles of shapes;
- angles on selected pieces of clipart;
- angles on photographs of familiar or real-life objects.

Case Study

Case study 7: 2-D shapes

For a group of Year 5 children who found aspects of numeracy difficult, I had planned a lesson introduction to recap the properties of regular 2-D shapes. I had prepared flipchart pages displaying a range of shapes, including some squares, some rectangles and three types of triangle. During the introduction, it became apparent that some children were uncertain about the properties of the triangles. It was necessary to address the issue before moving on.

Using the IWB, I created a new page on the flipchart and copied and pasted a selection of the triangles from previous pages onto one half. On the other half, through careful questioning of the children, we compiled a list of the properties of triangles. All took no more than a couple of minutes.

Selecting a metric ruler from the resource bank, I was able to invite some children to measure the lengths of the sides of the triangles and to annotate them on the board. Once this information was complete, we re-read the properties on the other half of the IWB. I gave the children a few moments to discuss with partners what they had learnt so far, and to apply this information to the problem of identifying the different triangles.

Through observing the discussions and listening to the children's findings, I was able to see that most of the children were much clearer about the properties and names of the triangles, providing a firmer footing for the subsequent activities.

Interactive rulers can be used for:

- drawing angles to be measured;
- measuring and drawing lines accurately in cm/mm;
- measuring the length of objects:
  - graphics and clipart can be used from the IWB's resources or copied and pasted from other programs or the Internet as required;
  - digital photos can be taken from around the classroom and measurements of these can then be taken on the IWB – older children could practise working out measurements to scale;
- measuring the dimensions of shapes to work out area, perimeter and volume;
- measuring the dimensions of shapes to work out some of their properties and then name them.

7. Handling data and using co-ordinates

Sorting and handling data can be carried out very easily on an IWB. You can create a simple Venn diagram by selecting two circles from the resource bank of shapes. How you use the diagram will vary depending on the lesson objective and the age and the ability of the children. Here are a few examples:

- Label one circle 'Four corners' and the other 'Not four corners'. Children could be asked to drag and drop shapes from a resource bank into the appropriate circle. This is a simple version of shape sorting. You could look at more discrete differences and similarities with older or more able children.
- Clipart images of various animals, modes of transport or items of clothing can be used for sorting activities based on a range of criteria from simple to complex.
- Children can sort a selection of numbers in a number bank according to certain properties – for example, odd or even, multiples of x or y, less than or more than x.
- Selecting a rectangle and then dividing it into four equal sections creates a Carroll diagram, which can be used alongside a Venn diagram to assist the children in sorting data.

You can create a graph or quadrant using two straight lines drawn using the line tool of an IWB, if you do not want any labels or numbers on the axes. It is quick and easy to set up and can be used by children of all ages. It is especially useful for simple bar charts; children can drag and drop a shape or item of clipart to represent a piece of data. If you require labels and numbers for axes, spend a little time looking at the appropriate resources section of your IWB's software. You are likely to find a range of graphs and quadrants already set up for use.

Using free downloadable resources

Some of the many free downloadable resources available to support the teaching of maths are listed in this section.

Interactive Teaching Programs

ITPs are produced by the DfES and available on their website. They have been produced to cover aspects of the mathematics strand of the Primary National Strategy. They range from number cards and counting activities using beads or number lines, to probability spinners and activities exploring remainders in division. These programs will save you a lot of preparation time.

Try one or two of these programs to start with. Get used to the way they look and work. One of their best aspects is that they are open ended: there is no prescribed way to use them. If you need a grid to practise direction or to work on symmetry, then the ITP on area is ideal for this. If you want to conduct an investigation into area and perimeter, or examine properties of 2-D shapes, the ITP on fixing points can be useful. You will find that, with a little lateral thinking, the same resource can be used in a number of different ways to support a very wide range of lesson objectives.

www.standards.dfes.gov.uk/primary/publications/mathematics/itps/

Number Gym

This website provides free maths programs that are similar in style to ITPs. They have similar applications. More complex versions of the programs can be purchased using your e-learning credits (eLCs).

www.numbergym.co.uk

Furbles

This program was written by Alec McEachran, who describes it on the website as 'an interactive probability and statistics application'. I have used this program for data handling, and ratio and proportion in Key Stage 2, although the appealing nature of the Furbles means that Key Stage 1 children will respond positively to it for sorting, counting and basic data-handling activities.

www.furbles.co.uk

The Numbers Game

This program is written by Chris Farmer, and is similar to the number challenge of the television programme *Countdown*. It is useful with older children and is excellent for mental maths skills and for explaining how a challenge was tackled.

www.csfsoftware.co.uk

Xnote Stopwatch and Timer

This was created by Dmitry Nikitin. While not specifically mathematically related, it is good for giving a class a visual reminder of how long they have left to answer a problem or complete a task.

www.xnotestopwatch.com

Using and editing photographs on the IWB to teach maths

Listed in the photocopiable website resources at the back of the book (pages 56–64) are a number of websites where you can download photographs free if they are being used for non-profit, educational purposes. Use these resources, as well as photographs of your own, to develop mathematical thinking. There follows a few ideas to get you going:

"So, the area of Manchester United's pitch is...?"

- Find shapes in everyday scenes.
- Use shapes to calculate area, perimeter and volume.
- Work with door numbers or speed-limit signs in all manner of ways, such as to develop number bonds or explore percentages/fractions of amounts.
- Look at symmetry, rotation and translation in patterns and shapes.
- Find parallel, perpendicular, bisecting or intersecting lines.
- Explore repeated patterns that can be used for arrays to work out multiplication problems.

Once you have captured an image on your IWB software, children can use the IWB to write about and annotate it. Using images in this manner is an engaging and captivating way to introduce a topic or lesson. You will find that the possibilities are endless.

Take your time with the ideas and suggestions in this chapter, perhaps starting by exploring some of the IWB tools mentioned, using a couple of ITPs and tapping in to the potential of one or two images. Then take a look at what the websites offer. As you progress, you will find yourself naturally thinking more about supporting your teaching with these methods. As your confidence with your IWB develops, so will your imagination and ideas.

Diary

Notes from the front line – the class teacher

Amazing, I can't believe that I managed to teach an interactive lesson and nothing went wrong today! I easily found the resources on my laptop now I have a sensible filing system. I loaded them onto the board and I got the children to use them with no problems whatsoever! It was so simple to create the pattern sequences, and the children really enjoyed highlighting the sequences in the photograph. It was great to see how eager Sam was to have a go. I don't think I have seen her like that for a long time. If this is what using the board effectively can do for her confidence, I'll use it a lot more!

I'll have to have a word with Neil and get him to take my old whiteboard down. I really don't think I need it any more – I never thought I would say that at the start of the term. There's plenty of room on the standard flipchart for the key things I need to have permanently up throughout the day and the old board is just taking up space that I could use to display some of the fantastic work the children have been coming up with recently.

Chapter 6 Science

As already mentioned, the IWB should not replace other hands-on resources and equipment. There is no substitute for children learning through their own experiences, and in science they should be allowed to conduct experiments and investigations. The IWB can be used to support such work and bring added elements of interactivity.

Easiteach: www.easitech.co.uk

Virtual Experiments: www.collinseducation.com

BBC Science Simulations: www2.sherston.com

Science Clips: www.bbc.co.uk/schools/scienceclips

www.smart-education.org

www.prometheanworld.com/uk

When teaching science with the IWB I use prepared resources more often than my own. Examples are purchased products such as Easiteach science, Virtual Experiments (available for Years 1 to 6) and Science Simulations.

There is a huge range of animations, flipcharts and programs freely available online that can be downloaded to support all aspects of the science curriculum. An example is the BBC's Science Clips section. Covering all the science units for ages 5–11, it is definitely worth looking at.

It is also worth looking at the SMART Board and Promethean websites. They have flipcharts you may be able to use or adapt to suit your requirements.

General uses for an interactive whiteboard

There are many opportunities for children to use images, still or moving, to assist their science work. For instance, digital photographs of animals in the locality can be displayed on the IWB and used to explore habitats, for sorting and classification and for presenting findings.

Because an IWB is able to project large images, I have taken the opportunity to introduce a science topic through a picture, or series of pictures. The children have been allowed time to discuss the image, then we have produced a mind map of what we already know about the topic. We have returned to the saved mind map later to see what we can add to it and what, if any, of the children's original thoughts and ideas were actually misconceptions.

www.visual-mind.com
www.mindjet.com/uk
www.smartdraw.com
www.mindmapper.com

There is software that enables you to produce mind maps on the computer easily. These can be made independently by children and then displayed on the IWB, or made as a group at the IWB. Try the websites in the margin to explore this.

Using digital video

There is a growing number of cheap and easy-to-use digital cameras on the market (the Intel Digital Blue Camera is an example). This resource can be set up to take time-lapse photographs of an experiment, or used to gather evidence for experiments. The quality of the image is not particularly high, so if you want a higher resolution picture for the IWB, you may do better using a more traditional digital video camera. With these, you can zoom in and capture close-up footage, so recording mini-beasts to display on the IWB is possible.

Searching on the Internet will yield a lot of footage that you would not be able to capture yourself. When preparing, type what you are looking for into a search engine and explore the results for something to meet your needs. For example, 'fireworks' produced a wide range of suitable film clips that I was able to use when focusing on light sources.

Google is a popular search engine that can also search for images, and Yahoo operates a similar search engine. If you are looking for something specific, putting quotation marks round a phrase will force the search engine to return results only if those words occur together. Your school's Internet filtering system may stop you using some image search engines because of the dangers of accessing inappropriate material. You can get round this by preparing at home if you have access to a computer. Otherwise you could use the safe search facility, an option often available under 'Preferences'.

www.google.co.uk
www.yahoo.com

"That's the slowest cheetah I've ever seen."

Another type of digital video camera available is the web cam. A web cam that relates to a particular theme provides you with an excellent resource for your IWB. The projected images enable the class to be transported anywhere in the world. (Web cams can be useful in other subjects than science, too.) When searching for a web cam on the Internet, be aware of the refresh rate of the camera that you find. This is the amount of time for the images taken by the web cam to appear. Ideally, you need a web cam that streams the images to allow you to watch the images in almost real time. Such web cams continually transmit images as they happen before the camera. This should guarantee that your class is not staring at the same picture for five minutes before seeing a new image.

It is not always easy to find a reliable web cam or one where the image is of a high enough quality. Start at the BBC's website; the content, from around the world, should be appropriate.

www.bbc.co.uk/webcams

Other resources

The IWB can be used in conjunction with a number of resources mentioned in Chapter 1 to support teaching and learning in science.

Digital microscope

A digital microscope allows the children to view objects and creatures in detail. Some can take still and moving pictures, enabling the children to capture and display details from experiments, and use them to present their findings to the class and in plenary sessions. Some of these microscopes can be set up and left for extended periods to take time-lapse or continuous footage. This can be saved onto a computer and viewed on the IWB at a later date.

Visualisers

These can be used to good effect in science, too. Groups of children can be shown large images on the IWB of close-up details of experiments, gaining a better understanding of the science involved. These images can be captured and saved so that you can refer back to them when the children are working independently, during a plenary or in a future lesson.

Data loggers

Data loggers have a lot to offer in science, used with or without an IWB. The children can use them independently of the computer to log such data as temperature levels or pulse rates. When reconnected to a computer, the software downloads the data, which can be converted into graphs and tables for use when writing up their experiments. These can also be displayed on the IWB to explore all manner of variables.

Additionally, data loggers can be used before a lesson to capture and graph data that you want the children to interpret. The graphs and tables produced can be displayed on the IWB for use in an introduction, before the children do a similar experiment. This provides an opportunity to develop the important Attainment Target 1 skills of the science curriculum – not always the easiest to teach or learn from with abstract data. Setting the data within the children's experience will help them to understand where the data have come from, which, in turn, will help them to interpret them in a more concrete way.

The Handling Data ITP can be used to produce basic graphs and tables that can be discussed and interpreted by children. Alternatively, the IWB software can be used to create simple bar graphs for Key Stage 1; and spreadsheet programs such as Microsoft Excel or Textease Spreadsheet can be used to set up graphs and tables to display on the IWB and used by those in Key Stage 2.

Diary

Notes from the front line – the class teacher

15 March

What a great resource the Internet is turning out to be! It's amazing that there are all these resources out there developed by teachers and shared on the web. It certainly makes preparation easier and that can't be a bad thing. I do feel a bit guilty, though, as I've just been downloading resources so far. I think it's about time to upload a couple of my flipcharts and give something back.

Every time I go online I find something new that I can use. I'm really looking forward to seeing how the children react to the science clips I found. SATs revision is never much fun for them, but hopefully they'll like the animations and the quiz will be a great way to assess their understanding.

Chapter 7
Foundation subjects

The foundation subjects can be supported in similar ways to those already discussed. I have tried to give ideas for subject-specific uses of the IWB and other resources, too. Hopefully, by now you will know most of the methods and options open to you, and be able to apply them to these areas.

Pictures and images

Pictures and images are excellent tools for starting off topics in the foundation subjects, or for initiating lines of enquiry for the children to follow independently or with support. Below is a case study that explores this application in geography.

Case Study

Case study 8: Local land use

Following a walk in two local environments, my Year 3 children shared evidence of positive and negative features that their group had noticed. In my planning, I had thought about how the IWB could work for this theme. I decided to give each group of children a digital camera, and asked them to gather photographic evidence to support their findings. They were very keen to find positive and negative aspects of local land use that other groups had not spotted. I downloaded these images and prepared a folder for each group's photographs. Over the next few days, the groups worked to plan a presentation of their findings, incorporating a showing of their photos on the IWB.

There was a definite sense of pride when they shared their evidence in the next session and the discussions that developed were very worthwhile.

Another good use of images in geography is to take photographs of the local area, and to use them in conjunction with maps. That gives the children the opportunity to associate the map with what they see when they are out and about. You could set up a flipchart page on the IWB with photographs of the specific sites around the edge and a map of the area in the middle. The children can use the IWB's tools to draw lines from the images to the appropriate points on the map. Younger children may need some help. You could use this to focus on journeys from home to school.

With older and more able children, I have used photographs to start off topics across all the foundation subjects and to develop effective enquiry skills. For example, in advance of a topic on the Tudors, I displayed an image of a Tudor rose in the middle of a flipchart page and gave the children a printout of the page. With a discussion partner, I asked them to jot down what they already knew on the subject and what they would like to know. We gathered this information on the flipchart page, the children adding some of the questions using the remote keyboard and the IWB pen.

Starting a topic in this way empowers the children, giving them ownership of the topic by focusing on what they want to find out – which normally matches your teaching and learning objectives. The record on the flipchart can be added to as the topic continues, with more detail and review of the questions. This approach works well for introducing RE themes. You can begin with an image, icon or artefact as the visual stimulus.

Video clips

Suitable video clips are easy to find and quick to download with a broadband connection. They can be used to support any subject. I have found simulations to assist aspects of design and technology projects. Using the IWB, you can discuss in detail how moving parts operate or how particular problems were overcome. If you copy an image onto a flipchart page, you can annotate it and use it as a reference point for designs or models that the children build.

I have used the Dogpile website to search for suitable video clips. This allows you to put in a theme of your choice. It will then search a number of different websites. You need to do this before the lesson so you can vet the content and find something appropriate. Once you have found a suitable video clip, follow these simple instructions to download it:

① On the search results page, right click on the file name you have chosen.
② Select 'Save Target As . . .'.
③ Choose the location in your 'My Documents' file that you would like to save the clip in.
④ Click 'Save'.

www.dogpile.com

Video clips are particularly useful in PSHE, art and PE:

- *PSHE*. I have used video clips and digital photographs of people conveying different emotions through body language to explore school scenarios that may have caused this feeling. This promotes exploration of how we can help people if they are experiencing a negative emotion. LDA's Feelings Photos can also be used on an IWB to explore emotions through natural and man-made landscapes.

Feelings Photos, LDA, 2005

- *Art*. I have used video clips to explore various drawing and painting techniques, and have scanned in images of the children's artwork to show how effects were achieved. Page 57 lists websites that are useful for art activities.
- *PE*. I have used video clips of professional gymnasts to demonstrate particular moves and jumps to children. You can give a lot of technical guidance using such clips. The children can incorporate this into their own routines and a digital video camera can be used to record their work. View this footage on the IWB and compare it with the original clip to highlight progress and points of development.

"That's got to hurt."

Video is also an excellent way to record work and progress in music. Video clips can be used as the stimulus for musical composition. I have shown video clips of musicians to point out the techniques of playing particular instruments and of playing in a small group. When the children have been working in groups on compositions, I have used a digital video camera to record their work in rehearsal stages and as a polished performance. We were able to save the rehearsal footage and refer back to it following the final performance to assess

The IWB was used to show performances to visitors, parents and other classes.

how the piece had developed and the children's skills had progressed. The IWB was used to show these performances to visitors, parents and other classes. We also used the soundtrack to accompany artwork inspired by the music that we had produced. Displaying this on the IWB while the music played made a real multimedia project. This can be applied to filmed sequences of dance and mime too.

Online resources

There is no single website that is ideal to support the foundation subjects. Think about what sort of resource you need, type a carefully worded search into a search engine, and see what comes up. This technique turned up the interactive Henry VIII mentioned in Chapter 3, as well as a host of history-related games and activities such as a cartoon Tudor jousting competition, quizzes and games. I have included some websites that I have found of use in each foundation subject on pages 54–58.

Chapter 8
Conclusion

I have put a lot of thought into how best to support and inspire you in your use of an IWB. I want to encourage you to make use of what I have shared with you when you are using your IWB. It is a tool that will only be as good as the person who uses it. I have given you the means to begin to use it or to refine your existing skills.

I have worked with many teachers who have had a range of emotions about the use of an IWB in their classroom. In time, even the most nervous and sceptical colleagues have admitted that an IWB allows them to teach and their children to learn in many new ways that they had not realised or appreciated were possible. I hope that you too are feeling that way now.

Hopefully, you will have been trying out the ideas and suggestions in this book as you have been reading – refining and adapting them to suit your needs and developing materials of your own, so that you have a range of really useful experiences and resources ready for your lessons.

Enjoy your IWB and enjoy your teaching. If you do, then so will your children.

Don't feel that you must be doing everything immediately. Go at a pace that you are happy with. If you are coming up with ways of using the digital camera at the moment and the children are benefiting from that, that's what matters most. Using digital video or downloading resources from the Internet can come later. We all develop at different speeds, and as long as you are willing to keep coming back to the ideas and suggestions here and to share and receive ideas from your friends and colleagues, you will make great progress.

Keep in the forefront of your mind that an IWB is interactive – it is meant for as many people as possible to work on and enjoy. The children I have spoken to all agree that having the IWB in the classroom makes their days more interesting and that they feel more positive about their progress. Most of all, they love the fact that they are learning alongside their teacher. They know that some of us are still developing our skills and confidence with an IWB. That makes them feel good because they can show us how to do things from time to time – and why shouldn't they?

Please, don't be afraid to make mistakes. Enjoy your IWB and enjoy your teaching. If you do, then so will your children.

Warning

When using the interactive whiteboard make sure of these things:

- You do not look directly into the beam of the projector.
- When in the beam, you do not look at the class or group for more than a few seconds.
- You keep your back to the beam of light as much as possible – stand outside the beam when talking to the class or group for a sustained period.
- Children are supervised.

© *How to survive and succeed with an interactive whiteboard* LDA Permission to Photocopy

Useful websites – Foundation Stage, Key Stage 1 and Key Stage 2

	General
F 1 2	**www.thelighthouseforeducation.co.uk** – The Lighthouse for Education is North East Lancashire's website, with a huge amount of resources.
F 1 2	**www.tre.ngfl.gov.uk** – The Teacher Resource Exchange is a database of resources and ideas for teachers that is easily searchable.
F 1 2	**www.bbc.co.uk/schools** – The BBC's schools' area is a good place to look for activities that support the curriculum.
F 1 2	**www.bbc.co.uk/webcams** – The BBC's web cam homepage. Start your journey around the world here.
F	**www.bgfl.org/bgfl/4.cfm** – The foundation stage index from the Birmingham Grid for Learning (BGfL) website.
2	**www.bgfl.org/bgfl/7.cfm** – Primary stage homepage from the BGfL website.
F 1	**www.enchantedlearning.com** – A huge American website with links to resources across a wide range of curriculum areas.
F 1	**www.firstschoolyears.com** – A well-resourced website containing Word, .pdf, interactive activities, web links, DfES and QCA resources.
2	**www.fossweb.com** – An American website useful for pictures and video clips as well as online resources.
F 1 2	**www.kented.org.uk/ngfl** – Kent's National Grid for Learning (NGfL) website with a host of useful web links to support teaching and learning.
F 1 2	**www.ngfl-cymru.org.uk** – The Welsh NGfL website has a wide range of resources for the whole curriculum.
F 1 2	**www.prometheanworld.com/uk** – Promethean's UK homepage has an excellent resource section, with links to appropriate flipcharts as well as web links to support the curriculum.
F 1	**www.riverdeep.net/products/downloads/free_downloads.jhtml** – An American website that includes plenty of free downloads to support thinking skills, language, maths and science.
F 1	**www.thebigbus.com** – Supporting literacy, numeracy, science and ICT, with free resources such as curriculum crosswords, handwriting page, test and worksheet makers.

Useful websites – Foundation Stage, Key Stage 1 and Key Stage 2

	Literacy
2	**www.bibliomania.com** – Contains more than 2,000 classic texts. You are likely to find what you need here.
2	**www.classicreader.com** – Out-of-copyright classic texts that can be copied and pasted.
F 1 2	**www.dk.com/schools** – Includes literacy resources and lesson plans linked to Dorling Kindersley's books, as well as free clipart and resource packs.
F 1	**www.dreambox.com/storybox/index.html** – Wonderfully illustrated online storybooks with the option to load the pictures in order to retell the story.
F 1 2	**www.fablevision.com** – Beautifully illustrated stories that can be downloaded and read on the IWB.
2	**www.gutenberg.org** – The original free eBook resource site, Project Gutenberg has been in existence since 1975 and boasts over 10,000 eBooks.
F 1	**www.ictgames.co.uk** – Games to support learners in literacy and numeracy.
F 1	**www.ladybird.co.uk** – Ladybird Books' homepage, with various stories, games and activities.
2	**www.literature.org** – Another website offering classic texts for use.
F 1	**www.ltscotland.org.uk/storybook** – A website full of activities for children, based on popular authors such as Frank Rodgers and Debi Gliori, and including video and audio clips of the authors reading the stories.
F 1	**www.naturegrid.org.uk/infant/bigbook.html** – Home of the Sebastian Swan big books, some of which have been translated into Welsh.
F 1 2	**www.richardatkins.lambeth.sch.uk/whiteboard_english.htm** – A school's website, with many resources.
F 1	**www.starfall.com** – This American site helps children to develop phonological awareness and reading skills.
2	**www.storiesfromtheweb.org** – This website is full of poems, short stories and extracts from longer stories by favourite authors. It also contains interviews with authors and gives children the opportunity to review books and send in their own work.

Useful websites – Foundation Stage, Key Stage 1 and Key Stage 2

Stage	Website
	Mathematics
F 1	**www.ictgames.co.uk** – Games to support learners in literacy and numeracy.
2	**www.johnandgwyn.co.uk** – Full of free downloads, most of the files here are teacher resources rather than interactive resources. Some of the random number generators are useful, as well as the link to a Countdown program.
2	**www.mathsonline.co.uk** – Free games dealing with shape and space objectives.
F 1 2	**www.mathszone.co.uk** – A collection of web-based resources to support all areas of the numeracy curriculum.
F 1 2	**www.numbergym.co.uk** – A range of freely downloadable activities.
F 1 2	**www.numeracysoftware.com** – Contains free numeracy downloads, including PowerPoint slideshows, My World screens, MSW Logo and Superlogo procedures.
2	**www.peda.com/poly** – Trial an interactive polygon program that allows you to show 3-D objects, and watch them open out into their respective nets.
F 1 2	**www.richardatkins.lambeth.sch.uk/whiteboard_maths.htm** – A school's website, with many numeracy resources. Mainly Key Stage 2 based, but some are suitable for Key Stage 1.
	Science
F 1	**www.angliacampus.com** – A range of images and animations to aid discussion of materials and their properties.
F 1 2	**www.bbc.co.uk/schools/scienceclips/index_flash.shtml** – A free resource that supports science teaching from the BBC.
F 1	**www.cchs.co.uk/tech-coll/primary/resources/ks1/electricity/activities.htm** – Flash activities that support children's understanding of electricity.
F 1 2	**www.crick.northants.sch.uk** – Use the Crick web link to access resources that support a wide range of science activities.
2	**www.edheads.org** – A website focusing on weather and natural forces.
2	**www.fossweb.com** – An American website of useful pictures and video clips as well as online resources.
2	**www.innerbody.com** – A website of information and images of the body's various systems, from skeletal to reproductive. The language is quite formal but would be useful for teacher-led sessions.
F 1 2	**www.naturegrid.org.uk** – From Kent NGfL, this website has online and downloadable resources.
F 1 2	**www.pet-educationresources.co.uk** – Contains a range of downloadable resources including photographs, games and worksheets to support the science curriculum.
F 1 2	**www.planet-science.com/under11s/index.html** – Set up for Science Year, this website has a wide range of activities for Key Stages 1 and 2.
2	**www.richardatkins.lambeth.sch.uk/whiteboard_science.htm** – A school's website with resources covering electricity, plants and the human body.

Useful websites – Foundation Stage, Key Stage 1 and Key Stage 2

	Design and technology
F 1 2	**www.primarydandt.org** – Run by the Nuffield Curriculum Centre, this website contains resources and freely downloadable resources to cover Key Stages 1 and 2 units of work in design and technology. Look in the Extra Resources and Archive sections for further materials.
	History
2	**www.ancientegypt.co.uk** – The British Museum's website on ancient Egypt.
F 1	**www.bbc.co.uk/schools/4_11/history.shtml** – The BBC's history section has a number of excellent websites to support the teaching of history at Key Stage 1. You are sure to find something to help.
2	**www.britishpathe.com** – News clips from 1896 to 1970; free preview quality downloads.
2	**www.oi.uchicago.edu/OI/MUS/ED/mummy.html** – Interactive Flash mummification resource.
2	**www.thebritishmuseum.ac.uk/compass** – Full of activities and resources to support children and teachers.
F 1 2	**www.topmarks.co.uk** – Educational website search engine with a number of links to support various aspects of Key Stage 1 history. Use the Subject and Age Range search facility to find appropriate resources.
	Geography
F 1	**www.bbc.co.uk/schools/barnabybear** – The BBC's barnaby bear website supports, but can be used independently of, the television programme of the same name, and is also linked to the appropriate Key Stage 1 QCA unit. Wide range of resources, as well as appropriate links.
2	**www.ordnancesurvey.co.uk/mapzone** – The Ordnance Survey has an interactive section aimed at developing children's mapping skills. Interactive map downloads, online activities and plenty of resources.
F 1	**www.scottish-island-shopping.com/coll/vtour/** – Panoramas of the Isle of Coll to examine.
2	**www.wateraid.org** – Ideal to use within the geography water unit, this website has a range of current news issues as well as plenty of teacher resources and a children's Learn Zone with games and real-life stories.
	Art and design
2	**www.eduweb.com/pintura/** – Children can play art detective as they try to solve cases based around famous artists and artistic styles.
F 1 2	**www.moma.org/destination** – The Museum of Modern Art in New York's child's website allows them to complete various activities based on modern works of art.
F 1 2	**www.tate.org.uk/learning/kids** – The Tate Gallery's homepage for activities aimed at children.

© *How to survive and succeed with an interactive whiteboard* LDA

Permission to Photocopy

	Music and sounds
2	**www.bbc.co.uk/northernireland/schools/4_11/music/mmm/index.shtml** – BBC music composition and exploration website.
F 1 2	**www.findsounds.com** – Search the Internet for sounds to download and use with your IWB.
F 1 2	**http://ngfl.northumberland.gov.uk/music** – A selection of resources to support music, especially The Music House and The Virtual Orchestra.
	PE
F 1 2	**www.byron.org.uk/School/Schemes/physed.htm** – More of a teacher preparation resource, offers free, differentiated PE units with examples in weekly/sequential units that follow the QCA and DfES recommendations.
F 1 2	**www.peprimary.co.uk** – A huge database of resources for primary PE. Some free downloads, but the bulk require paid registration. This can be bought using eLCs. Lesson plans for gym, dance and games from Reception to Year 6, supporting work/activity cards linked to the lesson plans, photographs for ideas for gymnastics and warm-up and cool-down activities.
	RE
F 1 2	**www.educhurch.org.uk** – Covering three churches, as well as links to mosques and synagogues, this website aims to support the QCA guidelines for RE.
F 1 2	**www.reonline.org.uk** – A website with a huge archive of searchable resources and weblinks. All religions covered.
	PSHE
F 1 2	**http://tre.ngfl.gov.uk** – Not a PSHE website, but the Teachers Resource Exchange has a database of ideas and website links that can be searched. Resources you may find useful include circle-time ideas, road safety, a link to the RSPCA, smoking and bullying.
2	**www.globalgang.org.uk** – Christian Aid's website has a wealth of resources and printable sheets to support children's understanding of key issues that affect others around the world. Regularly updated, with news, games and gossip sections to interest and inform.
F 1	**www.teachernet.gov.uk/pshe** – Searchable database on this website allows you to look for various types of resources to support the PSHE and citizenship aspects of the curriculum.

Subscription services

Key Stages	Website
F 1 2	**www.atschool.co.uk** – Supporting the Foundation Stage, Key Stage 1 and 2 as well as special needs across the curriculum, with web links, online activities and activities that can be printed out.
F 1 2	**www.espresso.co.uk** – Supporting the Foundation Stage; English, maths, science, art, music and PSHE at Key Stage 1, and English, maths, science, history, geography, PSHE, art, RE, music and French at Key Stage 2. There is a huge range of resources available, including video and audio clips, photographs, differentiated news articles, worksheets and weekly updates.
F 1 2	**www.gridclub.com** – Originally funded by the DfES, Grid Club offers a reasonable subscription rate, for which users receive access to a range of games and activities that support the whole curriculum as well as moderated chat rooms (accessible only to other Grid Club users), secure e-mail service and online forums to share problems or to ask questions.
F 1 2	**www.knowledgebox.com** – Supporting children from the Foundation Stage to Year 6, Knowledge Box currently covers literacy, numeracy and science with a range of images, video, interactive texts and resources.
F 1 2	**www.livinglibrary.co.uk** – An online reference library for children aged 5-11. Includes newspaper articles from four national newspapers, photographs, video clips, animations, audio clips and resources from six encyclopaedias written specifically for children.
F 1 2	**www.primaryonline.co.uk** – Supporting literacy, numeracy, ICT, history, geography and science across the key stages, with games and activities to play online.
F 1 2	**www.sparkisland.com** – Supporting literacy, numeracy and science for children aged 3-11, with games and activities played online.
F 1 2	**www.thebigbus.com** – Supporting literacy, numeracy, science and ICT for children aged 3-11, with free resources such as curriculum crosswords, handwriting pages, and test and worksheet makers.

© *How to survive and succeed with an interactive whiteboard* LDA

Permission to Photocopy

Interactive whiteboard resources and homepages

SMART Boards
www.smarteducation.org.uk – Complete the free registration for access to free SMART Notebook, Word, Excel and PowerPoint resources as well as 'How to . . .' files to help you get to grips with your SMART Board.
www.edcompass.smarttech.com – Download updates to the SMART Board software, free resources, lesson activities and 'How to . . .' files.
http://cardiffschools.net/~roelmann/whiteboard/smart2.html – Cardiff IT advisory team's website has a range of SMART Board resources.
www.smarttech.com – SMART Board homepage, based in Canada. Full of relevant and useful downloads, including updates to the SMART Notebook.

Promethean Boards
www.prometheanworld.com/uk – Promethean's UK homepage has a resource section with links to appropriate flipcharts as well as web links.
http://cardiffschools.net/~roelmann/whiteboard/activ2.html – Cardiff IT advisory team's website has a range of Promethean Board resources.
www.tlfe.org.uk/promethean/flipcharts.htm – Education website for North East Lincolnshire with Promethean resources for children from Foundation Stage up to Key Stage 4.

Miscellaneous
www.easiteach.co.uk – Not so much an IWB, but more of a program for creating interactive resources and lessons that can be used on any IWB, regardless of make, RM's Easiteach software has resources available for download here.
www.echalk.co.uk – A wide range of free, Flash activities mainly supporting literacy, numeracy and science.
www.ict.oxon-lea.gov.uk/whiteboards.html – Contains links and resources for teachers from Year 1 to Year 6.

Permission to Photocopy

School websites offering general resources

These support children across both key stages, unless otherwise stated
www.ambleweb.digitalbrain.com or **www.amblesideprimary.com** – Clicking on Resources takes you to resources that have been organised into Foundation, Y1/2, Y3/4 and Y5/6 sections. The second website address is the older version and contains many online resources.
http://atschool.eduweb.co.uk/toftwood/resources.html – A range of teaching resources for Key Stage 1 organised by subject and lesson objectives.
www.camelsdale.w-sussex.sch.uk – Camelsdale First School's website has a wide range of resources to support children from Reception to Year 3.
www.coxhoe.durham.sch.uk/Curriculum/Foundation%20Stage.htm – resource list for the Foundation Stage.
www.crick.northants.sch.uk – Use the Crick web link to access resources that support a wide range of activities.
www.hitchams.suffolk.sch.uk – Sir Robert Hitcham Primary School has a range of resource pages to support the whole curriculum.
www.jc-schools.net/ppt.html – An American website with lots of PowerPoint presentations.
www.richardatkins.lambeth.sch.uk – This website has resources to support a wide range of subjects.
www.snaithprimary.eril.net – A wonderfully illustrated primary school site with a wide range of useful resources.
www.woodlands-junior.kent.sch.uk – A wide range of games and activities available to support Key Stage 2 children.

Permission to Photocopy

Government and related organisations' websites

These support children across both key stages, unless otherwise stated.
http://tre.ngfl.gov.uk – The Teacher Resource Exchange is a database of resources. Easily searched.
www.becta.org.uk – The government's key partner in the development and delivery of ICT. This site contains a wealth of research, information and resources to support schools.
www.curriculumonline.gov.uk – The government website providing guidance and advice on how to spend eLCs.
www.naace.org – Set up to support schools in advancing education through the appropriate use of ICT, this website offers guidance and publications.
www.ncaction.org.uk – Offering exemplified materials for how ICT can enhance the curriculum, this website enables you to download and refer to a wide range of material.
www.ncsl.org.uk – The National College for School Leadership website contains advice and information on the strategic leadership of ICT.
www.nwnet.org.uk – The National Whiteboard Network website includes advice and links to resources supporting most curricular areas.
www.ofsted.gov.uk – This website has a wide range of research and information papers available.
www.qca.org.uk – Download up-to-date information and resources to support the delivery of the National Curriculum.
www.teachernet.gov.uk – Website for teachers, covering a wide range of topics from classroom resources to professional development.
www.tes.co.uk – *The Times Educational Supplement*'s homepage has online versions of a lot of its articles, as well as resources and forums.
www.standards.dfes.gov.uk – The Standards Site contains up-to-date materials, including the numeracy ITPs.
www.standards.dfes.gov.uk/primary – Homepage of the Primary National Strategy, it includes information and guidance on most things educational.

Miscellaneous teaching resources, utilities and resource websites

www.hedgehogs.gov.uk – This road safety website is full of games and downloads, including road safety adverts.
www.mape.org.uk/activities – This area of the MAPE website has a number of useful downloads.
www.schoolzone.co.uk – This is a great place to find out about software and web resources to support teaching.
www.xnotestopwatch.com – A useful timer to indicate the amount of thinking time children have, how long they have left to answer a question or how long they have to complete their work.
General teaching ideas and lesson resources
www.bgfl.org – The Birmingham Grid for Learning website: click on Activities Index and search activities by subject and/or key stage.
www.icteachers.co.uk – Teaching resources and subject management resources to support all areas of the curriculum.
www.ictgames.co.uk – Games to support infant learners in literacy and numeracy.
www.primaryresources.co.uk – Plenty of resources to support the curriculum. Don't forget to share your own resources on this site.
www.teachingideas.co.uk – This website has a lot of ideas that you may find useful.
www.teacherxpress.com – A useful website with links to hundreds of websites with relevance to teachers and teaching.
www.timetoteach.co.uk – A website supporting the whole curriculum, with plenty of free resources and links to websites.
www.topmarks.co.uk – This website has many useful links to support the whole curriculum. Includes a section devoted to IWB resources.

Videos, pictures, photos and clipart
www.clipart.co.uk – Free clipart that can be downloaded.
www.clipart4schools.com – Copyright-free clipart that can be downloaded.
www.freedigitalphotos.net – This website contains free photographs for commercial or non-commercial use.
www.freefoto.co.uk – Searchable database of copyright photographs. The main stipulation is that credit should be given to the website for any images used. This can be written in a small font at the bottom of the page.
www.freeimages.co.uk – Another site with free photographs. Credit should be given to the website for any images used. This can be written in a small font at the bottom of the page.
www.jurassicpunk.com – Download suitable film trailers to use in lessons. Trailers have been classified by the Rating Board of the Motion Picture Association of America (MPAA); view beforehand to ensure suitability.
www.morguefile.com – This website has a huge databank of photographs that can be used in class.

SEN
www.inclusive.co.uk – This website contains articles, resources and free downloads to support a wide range of inclusion and special needs issues.
www.priorywoods.middlesbrough.sch.uk – A Beacon special needs school with many free resources.
www.schooltrain.info – A teaching resource website focusing on deafness and on speech and language disorders. Contains links to teaching resources and other related resources and information.
www.sldonline.org/Kingsbury/Kingsbury.htm – Kingsbury Primary School in Lancashire is a special needs school with many useful links and resources on its website.